9-26

**CONTRIBUTIONS
OF WOMEN**

THE FIRST WOMEN WHO SPOKE OUT

by Nancy Smiler Levinson

Dillon Press, Inc.
Minneapolis, Minnesota

Library of Congress Cataloging in Publication Data

Levinson, Nancy Smiler.
   (Contributions of women)
   Bibliography: p. 128.
   SUMMARY: Presents the lives and achievements of six
women—Sarah and Angelina Grimké, Lucretia Mott, Sojourner
Truth, Elizabeth Cady Stanton, and Lucy Stone—whose
activities to earn rights for women took great courage as they
faced ridicule and scorn.
   1. Feminists—United States—Biography—Juvenile literature. 2. Abolitionists—United States—Biography—Juvenile
literature. [1. Feminists. 2. Abolitionists] I. Title. II. Series.
HQ1426.L48   1983   305.4'2'0922 [B] [902]   82-17685
ISBN 0-87518-235-6

Dillon Press, Inc., 500 South Third Street
Minneapolis, Minnesota 55415

Printed in the United States of America

Contents

The photographs are reproduced through the courtesy of the Burton Historical Collection, Detroit Public Library; Culver Pictures, Inc.; Friends Historical Society, Swarthmore College; The Granger Collection; and Sophia Smith Collection, Smith College.

Introduction

It is difficult to imagine a time when women in the United States were not allowed to voice a thought, express an opinion, or exercise civil rights. Yet a century and a half ago American women could not vote, speak in public, attend college, or own property. They were held to be weak-minded creatures who were fit only to be mothers and homemakers. And if they dared to question their place in society, they risked being scorned, ridiculed, and even attacked.

Yet a few women had the courage to speak out. They challenged the laws, customs, and prejudices that denied all American women justice and recognition. Most of them began their work in the temperance and antislavery movements. But they soon learned that their efforts would be fruitless unless they had the same rights as men.

Sarah and Angelina Grimké started the movement for equal rights. Condemned for their antislavery activities, they courageously advocated women's right to speak in public. Lucretia Mott continued their work by founding a women's antislavery society and by helping to organize the first women's rights convention. Sojourner Truth saw that both slaves and women were victims of injustice and inequality. She dared to claim freedom and independence for both groups. Finally, Elizabeth Cady Stanton and Lucy Stone began the campaign for women's suffrage. They clearly understood that rights could not be won nor laws be changed if women did not have the vote.

Each of these six women led remarkable lives. Each could lay claim to some individual achievement. But they are perhaps best remembered for what they began together: the American woman's long struggle for respect, freedom, and equality.

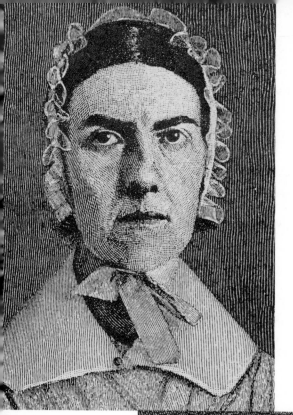

Angelina Grimké

Sarah Grimké

SILENT NO MORE

SARAH AND ANGELINA GRIMKÉ: Two sisters whose concern for the slaves in their native South led them to be the first female abolitionist agents in the United States. Sarah Grimké was the first American to write for publication on women's rights.

It was evening at last, and inside her bedroom young Sarah pressed her ear to the door. She waited to make sure no one in her large household was passing by. Then she stuffed a small piece of cloth into the keyhole. Next she put out the oil lamp, leaving only a bright, warm glow from the fireplace.

Sarah's slave stood in the room, clutching a book. She was supposed to be brushing and combing Sarah's long, dark hair. Instead, Sarah was going to give the little girl a lesson from her own speller. Teaching a slave to read and write was against the law in South Carolina, but eight-year-old Sarah was doing it anyway.

Even though the state law made no sense to her, Sarah knew that the lessons had to be given in secrecy.

This she had learned in the Sunday school provided for the children of the many Grimké family slaves. Sarah had seen how eager the youngsters were to hear the Gospel stories. When she asked why they couldn't be taught to read the Bible themselves, she was told that slaves had no mind for reading. Besides, her family said, slaves had no use for books. Moreover, if they learned too much, they would become restless and want their freedom.

Now, pretending that the slave was getting Sarah ready for bed, the two girls lay on their stomachs in front of the fire. Sarah opened the spelling book to the page where they had left off the night before.

Suddenly there was a shuffle of feet. Then before Sarah knew what was happening, they were discovered. The next thing she remembered was her father scolding her and telling her what a terrible crime she had committed.

Sarah felt that she had done no wrong, but it was useless to argue. Slavery was an accepted way of life among her family and their friends. No one but she seemed to question it. She could try to spare her playmate from punishment, though. And so she begged that the girl not be given a whipping.

Judge Grimké paced the floor as he made his decision. At last he said he would let the punishment go for now. But he made it quite clear to his daughter that she must never do such a thing again.

Although they were unable to study together after that, Sarah made sure that she and her slave remained close friends. When the black girl died two years later, Sarah wept as if her heart would break. Neither her parents nor her sisters and brothers could understand her grief. After all, they said, there were plenty of black children from whom she could choose another servant.

But Sarah could not be comforted. Slavery was horrible to her. What she saw of it as a child made her cry with fright. What she saw of it as a young adult made her feel sick with shame and guilt.

In time these strong feelings led her down a path no woman had dared to set foot on before. Both she and her younger sister Angelina helped to change the course of social history. Until they came along, no American woman had ever publicly spoken out against slavery or demanded the same rights as men.

Sarah Moore Grimké, the sixth child of John and Mary Grimké, was born on November 26, 1792. Her father was a judge, lawyer, and politician. Her mother was the daughter of a wealthy landowner and banker.

Like other rich South Carolinians, the Grimkés were also slaveholders. They used slaves to operate their large rice and cotton plantation, called Beaufort, and to run the town house they owned in Charleston, South Carolina. It never occurred to them that slavery might be wrong.

Sarah seemed to be a happy, cheerful child, but her diaries and letters reveal her to be otherwise. First, she never really fit in with the people around her. Despite the fact that she was surrounded by sisters and brothers, she felt lonely. She had no one with whom to share her private thoughts, especially her forbidden ones about the slaves.

Sarah was also unhappy with her education. "With me, learning was a passion," she once said, but as a girl, she was denied the right to learn. Like her sisters, she was given only a basic education in reading, writing, and arithmetic, along with lessons in manners, music, drawing, and needlework. These skills, her parents supposed, would teach her to be a lady and prepare her to manage a home for a husband and children.

Sarah admired her older brother Thomas and envied his schooling. She read all his books—from history to botany—but in a way her self-study program was almost worse than none at all. Instead of meeting her needs, it increased her appetite to learn more.

Judge Grimké wanted his sons to study law, and the young Grimkés often sharpened their minds in legal debates. Sarah joined in the lively talk and read the judge's law books in secret. When Thomas returned from Yale, where he had been studying law, she took a brave stand. She told her family that she wanted to study law, too. Sarah never told anyone what they said. Yet she referred to their refusal so often in the years to come that their words must have troubled her deeply.

On February 20, 1805, Mrs. Grimké gave birth to her last child. Now she had brought fourteen children into the world, three of whom had died while they were still babies. She was tired and weak. When Sarah asked if she could take care of the newborn, Mrs. Grimké agreed. It was Sarah who, as godmother, held the little girl in her arms when she was christened Angelina Emily Grimké.

Sarah spent hours on end with Angelina. They played, studied, and talked together. Through her older sister's love and guidance Angelina became a caring, sensible, and independent person.

By the time she reached her twenties, Sarah was thought of as an "old maid." During her teen years she had tried to fit into the carefree world of parties and balls, but it hadn't suited her. A young woman, she wrote in her diary, was only expected to be "a doll, a coquette, a fashionable fool."

When Sarah was twenty-six, Judge Grimké became ill, and he chose her to go with him when he went to Philadelphia for medical care. She stayed with her father and nursed him until his death. They had never before been so close, and the old man came to respect and depend on his daughter. Now that their roles were reversed, Sarah had the independence and dignity she had longed for. For the first time she saw the possibility of a different life for herself.

On returning home, Sarah saw the suffering of the slaves with renewed horror. Yet except for Angelina, no one else shared her feelings. Everyone in her family was either uninterested or too busy to talk at length with her. Besides, like most Southerners, they all found reasons for believing that slavery was right and proper.

Most people in the South were convinced that blacks were born to be slaves. In addition, they believed that slavery was essential to a healthy Southern economy. Without the labor of hundreds of thousands of unpaid slaves, cotton couldn't be grown and sold for a profit. And cotton was the source of the South's wealth.

But Sarah and Angelina saw that most slaveholders and their families had wealth beyond their needs. Of all the Grimké family and friends, the sisters seemed to be the only ones who viewed slavery as evil.

Sarah grew more and more withdrawn and depressed. Not knowing what to do about slavery, she felt useless and helpless. In the diary she kept at that time she wrote, "Every door of hope was closed."

She thought about Israel Morris, a man from Philadelphia, whom she had met on her way home from that city. He was a member of the Society of Friends and had told her a great deal about his religion. The Friends, or Quakers, as they were often called, based their faith on the Inner Light. They believed that it came from God and dwelled in the hearts of ordinary people. In letting themselves be guided by the Inner Light, they were more concerned with leading a pure, simple life than with worldly goods.

In a book Israel sent her, Sarah read what one Quaker had to say about slaveholders: "When I ate, drank, and lodged free-cost with people who lived in ease on the hard-labour of their slaves, I felt uneasy." Sarah was deeply moved by these words, and she asked her brother Thomas for more books about the Friends. He laughed and said that her long face suited the Quakers' plain dress.

In spite of his laughter, Sarah went on reading all she could find about the Friends and wrote to Israel, questioning him about his faith. The more Sarah learned, the more it appealed to her. As she turned to God, she felt less troubled. Soon she believed that God was calling her back to Philadelphia.

Sarah caused quite a stir when she made ready to go. People in Charleston were shocked that an unmarried woman would leave her home, family, and church. But Sarah ignored the gossip about her, and using the small amount of money she had inherited, she set off once again for the northern city. There she spent more than a year making herself ready to be accepted into the Society of Friends.

At first she was uncomfortable in the meetings, where people sat in silence until one of them was moved to speak. Those who had a gift for preaching were made ministers by their meeting. Lucretia Mott was a minister at the meeting Sarah attended. And Israel's sister Catherine, with whom Sarah was living, was one of its elders. Sarah had found a place where women were valued, and with encouragement she began to speak up at the meetings. At last she had a way of expressing her deepest thoughts and feelings.

On May 29, 1823, Sarah was accepted as a member of her meeting, and her diary notes that she began to wear the plain dress of a Quaker woman. She also wrote that becoming a Quaker seemed to be right for her, because it gave her a feeling of great peace.

Sarah often saw Israel Morris while she was living with his sister Catherine. He was a handsome widower with a family of eight children. But he was apparently in no hurry to remarry because he did not propose to Sarah until 1826, about eight years after they met.

Sarah had also fallen in love with Israel, but she struggled against her feelings and finally refused his offer. The only explanation she was able to give was that she didn't want to be anyone's wife. Yet every year thereafter she marked the date of his proposal on the calendar.

Meanwhile Angelina was growing up to be a poised, confident young woman. Like her older sister, she was more concerned with her spiritual life than with social graces. More and more she, too, became deeply troubled about slavery.

Angelina was especially upset by hearing people in South Carolina talk about how good life was for slaves there. Finally one day she could no longer sit politely and listen to such talk. A visitor in the Grimkés' home began bitterly complaining about how lazy and dishonest her slaves were. Her heart pounding, Angelina drew herself up and questioned the woman about the conditions of her slaves' lives. The woman was shocked. Turning on Angelina, she angrily said, "Never speak like that again to me."

Angelina could not let the matter go at that. "Truth," she answered, "cuts deep into the heart."

The sights and sounds of slavery also cut deeply into Angelina's heart. Every day she passed the workhouse where owners could send their slaves to be punished if they didn't want to do it themselves. One of those punishments was time on the treadmill. A slave's arms were tied to a bar above a revolving drum. As the drum turned, only the strongest men or women could keep their balance. Most slaves soon hung helplessly by the arms while the treadmill battered their legs at every turn. Angelina heard their screams as she gave Sunday school lessons to the workhouse master's little girl.

At home Angelina watched her brother Henry become hardened by the slave system. He often beat slaves who disobeyed him. One of them, a young boy named John, ran away rather than face another one of Henry's beatings. Running away only served to make Henry more angry, though. Angelina tried to reason with her brother by pointing out that he treated his horse better than he did his slave. Henry only replied that he would never beat a horse. Then, as Angelina put it, "I pleaded the cause of humanity." And it worked. For when John came home, Henry did not hurt him. Angelina had saved the boy from at least one cruel beating.

For some time now Angelina had been trying to do what she could about slavery in her home and her church. She found that her minister agreed with her views on slavery, but he would not preach a sermon on the subject. Angelina also went to a meeting of the church's elders, all of whom owned slaves, and asked them to take a stand. In a kindly way they tried to show her the error of her ways. Then she went to the members of the church, one by one, and made the same request. Some of them admitted that slavery was unjust and cruel, but, like the minister, none wanted to say so in public.

Following in her sister's footsteps, Angelina began going to the Quaker meeting in Charleston. Its membership had dwindled to two old men who were as puzzled by her attendance as she was by their silence. She could not understand why they were never moved to speak during the meeting. Finally, she learned that the two were not on speaking terms! One of them disapproved of the other owning slaves. In addition, he claimed that the slaveholder had cheated him in a business deal.

The leaders of the Presbyterian church Angelina belonged to became angry with her when she began attending the Quaker meeting. She was called before seven judges to answer charges that she was neglecting public worship, not taking Communion, and not keeping the promises she had made when she joined the church. She did not successfully defend herself, however, and the next day she received a letter expelling her from the church.

This action, together with her having lost hope that her family would change its ways, prompted Angelina to "escape from this land of slavery." In 1829 she left home to join her sister in Philadelphia. There she found a haven from her troubles and was overjoyed to find free black people living and working in the city.

Philadelphia had a long history of sheltering blacks who fled from slavery, in large part because the city had been founded by Quakers. Pennsylvania Quakers had condemned slavery as long ago as the 1680s. For years they had worked quietly to abolish, or do away with, slavery. Now they were being joined by other people of different faiths and backgrounds who also wanted to see slavery abolished.

The abolitionist movement was about to begin a phase marked by rapid growth and strong leadership. A date some historians use to mark its renewal is January 1, 1831. That is the date William Lloyd Garrison published the first issue of *The Liberator*, an abolitionist newspaper, in Boston. Garrison called for an immediate end to slavery and looked forward to the time when civil rights would belong to blacks as well as whites.

"I am in earnest—I will not equivocate—I will not excuse—I will not retreat a single inch," proclaimed the front page of *The Liberator*. And then in capital letters, Garrison declared, "AND I WILL BE HEARD."

Garrison's followers and other new abolitionists were gathering in strength and numbers. In 1833 they met in Philadelphia to found the American Anti-Slavery Society. Many people in the North and South opposed them, though. Southern slaveowners saw the growing movement as a threat to their way of life. Working people in the North thought their employers would use freed blacks as a cheap source of labor, leading to fewer jobs and lower wages.

As a result of this opposition, abolitionists—white and black—as well as free blacks found their lives in danger. In New York City state troops were called out to put down race riots, while in Philadelphia angry mobs burned down forty-five homes belonging to blacks. Abolitionist leaders and speakers were targets for stones, bricks, and rotten eggs.

Angelina began reading *The Liberator* and taking part in a local women's group, the Philadelphia Female Anti-Slavery Society. During the summer of 1835, while at the seaside home of a friend, she was distressed to hear that blacks were being attacked again in Philadelphia. And in her hometown of Charleston, a figure representing Garrison was hanged and then burned, with anti-slavery pamphlets piled at its feet.

Torn between fear for the abolitionists and hope for their cause, Angelina wrote a letter to Garrison. Without asking her permission, he published it along with her name in the next issue of *The Liberator*. From there it was picked up and reprinted by other abolitionist newspapers.

Angelina had never expected to see her name in print—and in such a place! Sarah scolded her. Her staid Quaker friends acted as if she had lost her wits. To their way of thinking, she was teetering on the edge of extremism.

Angelina, however, refused to turn back, and soon took an even more radical step. This time she wrote a long essay called *An Appeal to the Christian Women of the South*. In it she called slavery a crime against man and God. Further, she told the women of the South that they should not sit back and accept slavery. She suggested that they speak their minds to their husbands, fathers, and brothers. Those women who owned slaves should free them, she claimed, and pay them wages. At the very least they should teach slaves to read and write, even if they had to break the law to do so.

When the essay was published, it had far-reaching effects. It was widely advertised by the American Anti-Slavery Society, and parts of it were reprinted in *The Liberator*. Garrison's newspaper also printed letters from readers who were grateful for the essay. A special edition of the appeal was published in England. But in Charleston, South Carolina, officials burned any copies of the essay that reached the post office there. And the Charleston police made it known that Angelina Grimké was forever banned from the city of her birth.

Now Angelina felt ready to accept the antislavery society's invitation to come to New York City for training as a speaker. Because she was a woman, the society didn't think she was fit to speak in public places. However, the group's leaders believed that she might meet the needs of sewing circles and other domestic audiences.

Sarah tried to talk Angelina out of going, but Angelina insisted. Speaking, she said, relieved her mind. Finally Sarah gave in and agreed to go with her because, she said, "We have always thought and wept and prayed together."

Since Sarah accompanied Angelina, the antislavery society decided that she, too, would be helpful to the movement. So along with some forty others, both sisters were trained in speaking methods. The only women in the three-week course, they were drilled in debate by some of the best speakers in the nation. They met William Lloyd Garrison and were taught by Theodore Weld, a spellbinding orator and an organizer of the antislavery society. Sarah became fully caught up in the cause. "It is so good to be here that I don't know how to look forward to the end of such a feast," she wrote.

After the feast was over, the sisters were equipped

for meeting far greater challenges than sewing circles. The numbers of women who flocked to hear them in New York City made parlor talks impractical. As a result, they moved to a church meeting room and then to the pulpit itself.

"I would not give up my abolition feelings for anything I know," Sarah wrote to a friend. She first expressed these feelings in print in *An Epistle [(Letter)] to the Clergy of the Southern States,* published in 1836. In it she used her love of the law to point out contradictions between Christian teachings and slave state laws. What a furor the letter caused! How dare anyone speak in such a manner to men of God? people said. And a woman yet!

Now Sarah was as deeply involved in controversy as her sister, and they were both astonished at the road they had traveled. Yet an even more extraordinary year followed. For in 1837 the sisters began a lecture tour of New England. Wendell Phillips, an abolitionist leader, later claimed that this tour made the greatest contribution to the antislavery movement.

In town after town the sisters tried to convince their growing female audiences of the truth of human bondage. Angelina made a plea on behalf of the black women who were slaves. "They are our sisters," she told her listeners, "and to us as women, they have a right to look for sympathy with their sorrows and effort and prayer for their rescue."

Some of the Grimkés' stories were so shocking that Northern women found it difficult to believe them. But they became popular speakers, and their listeners filled the meeting halls of New England towns. Working-class women walked up to eight miles to hear them.

Although Sarah and Angelina were popular with some audiences, others treated them as freaks. They began to be viewed as such curiosities that a handful of men started attending the lectures. In Lynn, Massachusetts, a textile mill town, several men entered the meeting hall and stayed for the whole program. This was the first time the Grimké sisters spoke before a large "mixed" audience of men and women, and it shocked people.

Then Angelina did something even more shocking— she challenged two men to a debate. People could not believe that she dared to do this. For at that time only men were supposed to speak in public or engage in a debate.

The incident that prompted the debate occurred in the small town of Amesbury, Massachusetts. Two young men in the audience announced that they had visited the South. Slavery, they declared, wasn't nearly as bad as the Grimkés held it to be.

Without a moment's thought, Angelina challenged the men to debate the issue. They agreed, thinking she would be easy to defeat. But they were quite wrong. For when they tried to show that the Bible approved of slavery, she countered with a strong biblical argument of her own and handily won the debate. Yet the editor of the *Amesbury Morning Courier*, fearing for the morals of his readers, refused to print what had been said.

Now even the people who had sided with the sisters began to criticize them. Their fellow Quakers denounced them for being involved in worldly affairs. The abolitionists asked them to play down their views, fearing that their lectures might damage the antislavery cause. But there was no turning back. "We are willing to bear the brunt of the storm," Angelina said.

Angelina was the better speaker of the two sisters, but each of them gave lectures on the tour. In addition, Sarah spent a good deal of time in reading and study. She was also becoming aware of the people who worked in New England's mills and factories. A quiet, keen observer, she took special notice of the poor working women and their children. She saw how they worked from dawn till dusk for much less pay than a man. And by law even the money the women earned belonged to their husbands. It was no wonder then that many of the women who were drawn to the Grimkés' lectures felt that their lives were no better than those of the slaves.

Sarah and Angelina's speeches made them the most famous women in New England for a time. But as their fame grew, so did opposition to their ideas and activities. In July 1837 the official organization of Congregational ministers in Massachusetts warned against them in a public letter. It never mentioned the sisters by name, but they were clearly the "dangers" of which it spoke. A woman's need to depend on man was her strength, the letter said. "But when she assumes the place and tone of a man as a public reformer, our care and protection of her seem unnecessary . . . and her character becomes unnatural."

This letter was read in every Congregational church in the state. One minister later remarked that he would rather "rob a hen-roost than hear a woman speak." Others threatened to expel their members from the church if they listened to the Grimkés speak.

Sarah responded to the clergy by writing a letter of her own. It was later included in the first book on women's rights published in the United States, *Letters on the Equality of the Sexes*. In this revolutionary book

Sarah called for women to be given the same educational opportunities as men and demanded equal pay for equal work. She also cited laws that were unfair to women. But most important she challenged the idea that women were inferior to men. "How monstrous is the doctrine that woman is to be dependent on man," she declared. For God had meant men and women to be equals. Therefore men should "take their feet from off our necks, and permit us to stand upright on that ground which God designed us to occupy."

Sarah's reply to the *Pastoral Letter* made it difficult for her and Angelina to continue their antislavery lecture tour. But they would not be silenced. When the churches were closed to them, they spoke in town meeting halls. If a hall was denied them, they found a barn. From August through October of 1837 they gave five or six talks a week, each one in a different town.

The tour ended only when they were too ill to go on. Sarah came down with bronchitis, and soon afterwards typhoid fever struck Angelina. Theodore Weld, the man who had trained them, was especially upset. Throughout the tour Sarah and Angelina had looked to him for advice and encouragement. Now he wrote them from New York City and begged them to give up their work. "Save yourselves for the slave, for human rights, for woman's rights," he pleaded.

Angelina had long been in love with Theodore, but he never seemed to have any interest in her. In fact, he had vowed never to marry until the slaves were free. Yet just when she despaired of ever winning his heart, he confessed his love for her in a long and emotional letter.

More letters between them followed, as they tried to come to terms with their feelings for each other. Theodore was so troubled by what was happening to him that he lost weight and was unable to sleep. Both he and Angelina were utterly confused by what was happening to them.

In time, though, they were able to resolve their doubts about love and marriage. It was possible, they decided, to give their hearts to God and yet still love each other. Moreover, they need not give up their reform work if they became husband and wife. Finally, they could ask Sarah to live with them once they were married.

Angelina and Theodore were married on May 14, 1838, in Philadelphia, Pennsylvania. They followed no ritual, and instead exchanged vows that they made up on the spot. Theodore added a few sharp words against the idea that a woman's property belonged to her husband upon marriage. Prayers by the pair followed, and then two ministers—one black and the other white—gave their blessings to the union. It was a strangely modern ceremony and one perfectly in tune with their beliefs.

Two days later Angelina gave a speech in a brand-new antislavery hall in Philadelphia while an angry mob pelted the windows with stones. It was her last public appearance for many years. Although the sisters continued to work hard for abolition and to practice their antislavery principles in daily life, they fell back from the front lines of the battle.

The sisters' first real home was a small and rather barren house on the Hudson River near New York City. There they grappled with the problems of housekeeping for the first time. Cooking was one new task that didn't take much effort. They were great believers in the health diet prescribed by Dr. Sylvester Graham, the inventor of the Graham cracker. The diet he recommended consisted mostly of rice and molasses, stewed beans, raw fruits, and nuts.

Among the many visitors to the Weld's new home was Elizabeth Cady Stanton, who had just married a friend of Theodore's. Elizabeth found that she had much in common with the Grimké sisters. She shared their passionate concern for women's rights. In time she would become one of the foremost leaders of the American women's movement. More than fifty years after her visit, she would use Sarah's argument for the equality of the sexes in one of her own books, *The Woman's Bible.*

About a year and a half after her marriage, Angelina gave birth to the first of her three children. Motherhood did not come easily to her, however, and her already frail health began to decline. Her letters and those of her family do not reveal exactly what the problem was, but she clearly suffered great pain at times.

Because of Angelina's ill health, Sarah once more took on the role of mother. She loved the Weld children—Charles, Theodore, and Sarah—deeply. In a dark moment she wrote, "I know not what would have become of me but for Angelina's children."

Sarah's contentment as a homemaker did not last, however. By the age of sixty she became restless and unhappy. She did not know where to turn or exactly what she wanted to do, but she decided to leave the Weld's home.

Yet it was not long before she felt lost and homesick, and especially longed to see the Weld's children. Angelina was not sure she wanted her sister to return, though. She was grateful for what Sarah had done, but she did not want to share her family any longer. But in the end she invited her sister back, and Sarah returned.

Not long afterwards the Welds moved to a new cooperative community near Perth Amboy, New Jersey. The Raritan Bay Union, as it was called, was intended to be a model community, financed and built by its members. Unfortunately, the plan failed after a couple of years, but the school that drew the Welds to Raritan Bay became a reality. Known as Eagleswood, this school was attended by both blacks and whites.

The Eagleswood School had a rich, varied educational program and a large teaching staff. Theodore was its principal, Angelina gave instruction in history, and Sarah taught French and acted as housemother. Intellectuals and social reformers of all sorts, including those working for abolition and women's rights, came to speak there.

Sarah, Angelina, and Theodore were still living and teaching at Eagleswood when the Civil War broke out. As Southerners and lifelong pacifists, Sarah and Angelina hated to see it begin. And yet they saw the war as the only way left to end slavery.

Along with Theodore, the two sisters were impatient for the North to proclaim emancipation—the freeing of the slaves. Theodore had ruined his voice while campaigning against slavery in the 1830s. Now he risked it once more to go on a speaking tour designed to win support for emancipation. Angelina did her part by defending the war before a national convention of American women. She knew that the war was going to destroy her homeland. Yet she told the women that "as a South Carolinian, I am bound to tell the North, go on! go on! Never falter, never abandon the principles which you have adopted."

During the war Sarah and the Welds moved to

Hyde Park, Massachusetts, near Boston, and opened a school. It was at Hyde Park that Sarah and Angelina spent the rest of their lives, and there that they welcomed two unexpected additions to their family.

A few years after the war, Angelina found out that two young men by the name of Grimké were going to a school for blacks in Pennsylvania. They turned out to be the sons of Henry Grimké and Nancy Weston, one of Henry's slaves. Henry had died years before, and the boys, after periods of enslavement, had made their way to the Lincoln School in Pennsylvania.

Sarah and Angelina opened their hearts and their home to their newfound nephews. Thanks to their kindness and support Archibald Grimké became the first black person to graduate from Harvard Law School. He went on to serve as a vice-president of the National Association for the Advancement of Colored People and wrote many articles on black rights. After earning a divinity degree from Princeton Theological Seminary, his brother Francis became a well-known minister. He also served as a trustee of Howard University. Both of them credited their aunts with having inspired their work.

The next generation of women were also inspired to carry on the struggle for their rights by the Grimkés' example. Over the years the sisters had formed firm friendships with the leaders of the women's movement. They continued to take part in women's rights meetings, and at those gatherings they were treated with great respect by the younger women. They were recognized as having taken the first courageous steps on the path that so many others were now following.

Sarah died in 1873 and Angelina six years later. For

most of their long lives, they had been engaged in a double battle, fighting against the tyranny of both sexual and racial prejudice. As they made their way toward their own freedom, they unlocked the doors for those who followed them.

LED BY AN INNER LIGHT

LUCRETIA MOTT: A deeply devout Quaker minister who has been called the "soul and the spirit" behind the women's rights movement.

"I hope that no person will be alarmed by a little appearance of danger," Lucretia Mott said, standing before the Convention of Anti-Slavery Women. She was having a hard time keeping order and calm at the gathering, which was being held in Pennsylvania Hall in Philadelphia. Just yesterday, Angelina Grimké Weld had given one of her most moving speeches to the sound of breaking glass, as a wild proslavery crowd outside the hall shouted insults and hurled stones at its windows. Now, as Lucretia tried bravely to continue, the women could hear rumblings of an even larger and angrier mob growing in the street below.

The business before the convention was to decide whether to follow the mayor's advice and ask black women to leave the meeting in order to keep the peace. Lucetia asked her listeners to vote no, and they did. Then to show their unity, the women left the hall in pairs—one black woman arm in arm with a white woman. The mayor came to lock the door and then left the hall unguarded.

Armed with torches and axes, the proslavery mob broke into the first floor offices and ripped books and papers from the shelves. Billows of smoke poured from the broken windows as the hated antislavery books and pamphlets were set ablaze. No one, not even the firemen, made a move to put out the fire. They merely sprayed their hoses on the neighboring buildings to keep the fire from spreading along the street.

Outside, Lucretia and her friends watched in horror as the hall became engulfed in flames. Freedom-loving abolitionists had just built it at great expense. Pennsylvania Hall was meant to be a place where American citizens could go to discuss liberty and equality. But in this city, chosen to cradle the Liberty Bell, the mob rejoiced as it watched the building burn to the ground.

Although there was no legal slavery in Pennsylvania, the crowds were on the side of the slaveowners. They had convinced themselves that blacks were not meant to be free. Also, they saw the issue of slavery in economic terms. A sudden end to slave labor, they thought, would be bad for business and farming, and men and women who worked in low-paying jobs felt especially threatened.

Underlying both these views lay a deep fear that blacks and whites would marry and raise children. Many whites thought that such marriages would somehow make their race less pure. In the North any show of friendship between blacks and whites could trigger a riot when racial prejudice ran high. Two days before the Convention of Anti-Slavery Women blacks and whites had been invited to the wedding of Angelina Grimké and Theodore Weld. Allowing the two races to come together as equals added to the anger of the whites who later burned down the new hall.

In Philadelphia and other Northern cities, proslavery forces were using any means they could to break up antislavery meetings like the one organized by Lucretia. Yet despite the mounting dangers, she went on with her work. She and her husband often risked their safety as they helped slaves who were escaping on the Underground Railroad. Late at night, in hushed and hurried secrecy, the Motts fed, clothed, and sheltered runaways in their own home, while arranging for the fugitives to continue their escape.

At the time she led the women out of Philadelphia Hall on that May evening in 1838, Lucretia was used to conducting meetings and making speeches. She had been a Quaker minister for almost twenty years. She had also been one of the founders of the Philadelphia Female Anti-Slavery Society after the newly formed American Anti-Slavery Society made it clear that it would not admit women as members. This gentle, modest preacher has been called the "soul and the spirit" behind the women's rights movement that was still to come.

The fact that Lucretia Mott became an educated woman, a leader, and a gifted speaker was due in large part to her having been born to a Quaker family. The meetinghouse where they went every Sunday on the windswept island of Nantucket was as plain as the gray gowns and black bonnets of the women. The worshipers sat on bare wooden benches—the women and girls on one side of the aisle and the men and boys on the other. There was no altar, no choir, and no pulpit. Instead, there was only a plain bench on which the elders and the ministers sat, facing the meeting.

The elders were in charge of the conduct of the members during the meeting and in their daily lives as well. The ministers were ordinary people who preached so well that they were singled out for special notice. Because any Quaker could become a minister, Lucretia grew up believing that men and women were equal in the eyes of God.

The island of Nantucket, where Lucretia was born on January 3, 1793, was a major shipping center off Cape Cod in Massachusetts. Ships left its busy harbor for all parts of the world. While the men were away on long voyages, the women supported themselves and their families. Lucretia's mother Anna ran a little shop in her front parlor when her husband Thomas Coffin, a ship's captain, was at sea.

Lucretia was the second child in a family that eventually included five girls and one boy. Yet even as a young girl, she acted like a typical big sister, ordering the other children about and carrying out many household tasks. She dutifully set the breakfast table, brought water in from the pump in buckets, and washed the dishes each day before school. In the evening she mended clothes or wove rags into rugs.

Lucretia wasn't *always* dutiful. She had a sharp temper and sometimes talked back to her elders. At her "cent" school, where pupils paid a penny a day for their lessons, she grew impatient with students who didn't learn as quickly as she did. As a result, she felt uneasy when someone spoke about proper Quaker behavior at meeting. Questions asked of all members—Dost thou control thy temper? Art thou patient? Dost thou practice plainness of speech and clothing?—made her wriggle on her bench.

One Sunday a woman was moved to tell the Bible story of Joseph during the meeting. Lucretia stopped wriggling and really listened. According to the story, God had given Joseph the strength he needed to carry on with life after his brothers had sold him into slavery in Egypt. Lucretia wanted to be strong, too, like the early Quakers who had risked everything to follow the guidance of their Inner Light. Through it, they believed, God spoke directly to each human heart. Like them, Lucretia felt prompted by something deep within her to be dutiful.

At home afterwards she eagerly looked for an outward way to show her inner change. Certainly her gray and white dress could not be made more simple. Neither could her little starched white cap. Then she looked down at her shoes. Fastened on their toes were blue bows, a gift from an uncle. Without further thought, she snatched up a pair of scissors and snipped the bows off.

Lucretia had her chance to do her duty and then some when Captain Coffin was able to buy his own whaling ship and set off on a long sea voyage. He had put all of the family's money into the purchase of the *Trial,* and now Mrs. Coffin had to re-open her shop, despite having several children to care for. Not only did Lucretia have more household chores, but when her mother traveled to the mainland to trade goods in Boston, she was left in charge of the shop.

Two years stretched into three, and still the *Trial* did not appear in Nantucket's harbor. The family was beginning to fear that Captain Coffin had been lost at sea when he appeared at their front door one day. The *Trial,* he told them, had been seized by a Spanish man-of-war off the coast of South America. As a result, the Coffins had no ship and little money.

Captain Coffin decided to quit the seafaring life. With funds from the sale of furs he had shipped to China before the *Trial* was taken, he bought into a business partnership in Boston. His office was tucked among the warehouses on the wharf, and there he bought and sold goods that the ships brought into the harbor.

In the new city Lucretia no longer had to pay her teacher for each day's lessons. Yet she couldn't understand why people said she was attending an "equal" school. For while the boys went to school all year round, the girls were admitted only for a few months. And while the boys studied Latin and Greek, the girls were only taught to sew and cook.

When Lucretia was thirteen, Mr. and Mrs. Coffin decided to send her and her younger sister Elizabeth to a Quaker school in Nine Partners, New York. Students at this school received a fine education, but they had to obey strict rules. Girls and boys lived and studied in different parts of the big building. They had separate classrooms and playgrounds and were not even allowed to speak to each other.

Most of the time Lucretia followed the school's rules, but now and then she felt she had to stray. One time she heard about a boy who was being punished by being locked in a closet for a whole day. Believing this to be unjust, Lucretia sneaked into the boys' side of the school and slipped the poor fellow a piece of buttered bread underneath the door.

Lucretia learned a great deal during her two years at Nine Partners. In addition, she first came to feel strongly about slavery. Up until that time she had known little of the suffering it caused. There had been no slaves on the tiny island of Nantucket, where she was born, nor in Boston. Now she learned that slavery was legal in New York State, and that many Americans were deeply involved in the slave trade.

On the wall of Lucretia's classroom hung a picture of a slaveship packed with wretched people who had been kidnapped from their African homeland. Lucretia read about the horrors of their voyage in Thomas Clarkson's *Essay on Slavery*. Clarkson told of slaves being tortured, raped, starved, and even thrown overboard so that shipowners could collect insurance money on their human cargo. She also listened to Elias Hicks, a founder of the school and a member of the school committee. Hicks was a fiery preacher who was trying to stir his fellow Quakers to see the wrongfulness of owning slaves.

Lucretia proved to be an excellent student, and at the end of her second year, she was offered a job assisting the girls' head teacher. It was without pay, but she received free room and board. The following year she was offered a "raise" in the form of free tuition for her sister Elizabeth.

Meanwhile, Lucretia somehow got a glance at the school's accounts. To her surprise and disgust she learned that the teacher she was helping was not being fairly paid. In fact, the woman earned less than half the salary of the school's male teacher, even though she was older and had been teaching longer. Lucretia made up her mind that when the time came, she would demand what her work was worth.

She knew and liked the male teacher in question. He was James Mott, the brother of her best friend. She had visited the Mott home during a school vacation, and now she was taking French lessons with James and a few of the other teachers. Just as their friendship had begun to turn to romance, however, she was asked to join her family in Philadelphia. Mr. Coffin had opened a nail factory there and business was booming.

In the months that followed, the young couple made their feelings for each other known and their families agreed to a marriage. James moved into the Coffins' home and joined the business. On April 10, 1811, in a simple Quaker ceremony, Lucretia and James held hands and recited their vows.

A friend later remarked, "If James and Lucretia had gone around the world in search of a mate, I think they would have made the choice which heaven made for them." They were to remain husband and wife for fifty-seven years.

The future, which had intially looked so hopeful, turned bleak following the birth of Anne, the first of the Motts' six children. Business fell off during the War of 1812. The nail factory and shop failed under a mountain of debts, and James looked in vain for work elsewhere. Then Mr. Cofin died of typhus in 1815. Once more Mrs. Coffin opened a shop and James, inspired by her success, tried one of his own two doors away. He must have lacked his mother-in-law's sharp management skills, though, for his shop failed, and James cast about for jobs as far away as New York City.

Several months after her son Thomas was born, Lucretia found a way to help her family as well as put her training at Nine Partners to good use. Her cousin

Rebecca had been hired to open a Quaker school for the Pine Street Meeting, and she took on Lucretia as her assistant. Beginning with four students, the school grew to have a total of forty.

The Motts were dealt yet another blow one April day in 1817. Lucretia and Thomas came down with high fevers. Dazed and sick, Lucretia sat at her little boy's bedside and helplessly saw him die. Many years later, when she was an old woman, one of her family asked why she became a preacher. Tears came to her eyes even then as she answered that Tommy's death had led her into the ministry.

Lucretia's preaching career began at the Twelfth Street Meeting, when she rose to her feet and said a short prayer. Her clear voice and sincerity must have seemed out of the ordinary, for her listeners asked her to speak again when she felt she had a message to give.

The Society of Friends had no formal ritual by which a person became a minister. Instead, the Quarterly Meeting of several congregations issued a "recommending" that someone had a gift for the ministry.

Lucretia's calling was acknowledged in this way in 1821, when she was twenty-eight years old. It was a high honor for one so young, and a turning point in her life. "Surrounded with a family and many cares, I felt called to a more public life of devotion and duty," she wrote in her diary.

In the years that followed Quakers began to disagree about the nature and practice of their faith. Many of them were influenced by the views of Elias Hicks, the preacher who had visited Lucretia's geography class at Nine Partners. He felt that many big-city Quakers were losing sight of the original doctrine of the Society of

Friends. No longer did they lead simple, thrifty lives. No longer did they place their trust in the Inner Light that could lead directly to God. Instead, Hicks believed that they were following the teachings of other churches and the customs of worldly folk.

After many debate-filled gatherings and a good deal of soul-searching, Hick's followers split away from other Quakers. Known as Hicksites, they organized their own meetings for worship. Lucretia and James decided to leave her beloved Twelfth Street Meeting, and gather with other Hicksites in Carpenters' Hall. She was a valued leader of the new group and was chosen clerk of the Philadelphia Women's Yearly meeting in 1830.

Lucretia and James soon had to make another important decision. This time it concerned joining a movement not to buy the products of slave labor, such as sugar, rice, cotton, and even paper made with cotton rags. Lucretia was opposed to slavery and felt she should take part in this boycott. She stopped buying slave-produced goods and spoke out for the boycott at her meeting.

James found it more difficult to join the boycott. He was now doing well in the wholesale business, and he dealt in slave-grown cotton. Slowly, however, he came to believe that he must risk his family's well-being and try to sell wool instead of cotton.

By 1830 both Motts were wholly committed to abolition in their public and private lives. Lucretia felt so strongly about the issue that she began giving antislavery lectures. She also joined forces with other abolitionists, such as young William Lloyd Garrison.

In 1833 Lucretia was one of six women invited to be observers at the founding of the American Anti-Slavery

Society. None of them was invited to be members because a woman was not supposed to take part in public affairs. Lucretia felt comfortable, however, in suggesting several changes in the Declaration of Sentiments that the men were drawing up. When the time came to sign it, several abolitionists refused. Their businesses, their reputations, and even the safety of their families were at stake. "If our principles are right," Lucretia prodded them, "why should we be cowards?" After more discussion, she said softly, "James, put down thy name!" Without hesitating, he wrote out his signature, the first one on that historic declaration.

Five days later Lucretia called a meeting of her own to set up the Philadelphia Female Anti-Slavery Society. Eighteen women were brave enough to attend it. A peculiar problem occurred in the Quaker schoolroom that evening, though. It was considered so outrageous for a woman to lead a meeting that none of the eighteen—not even Lucretia—felt she could dare to take charge. Not until one member, a black woman, ran down the street to get her husband to preside did the session get underway.

After the first meeting, the little group of women never felt they needed a man to take charge. In fact, they found that they could not only discuss their ideas but act on them. They wrote stacks of letters to Congress. By selling pin cushions and aprons, they raised money to aid poor black people and to send out lecturers. And amid loud cries of protest and threats of destruction they even managed to open a school for black children.

In 1840 the World Anti-Slavery Convention was held in London, and both James and Lucretia Mott were named to attend it as delegates from Pennsylvania. Full of high hopes, they sailed for England that spring. But those hopes were dashed for Lucretia as soon as she arrived. She found out that women were not allowed to take part in the convention. All they could do was sit in the balcony and watch.

This insulting, frustrating experience led to the first Woman's Rights Convention in the United States. For in London Lucretia met a young woman who was equally angry at having been sent to the balcony. The woman, a bride on her honeymoon, was Elizabeth Cady Stanton.

At the dinner table in the boardinghouse where they were staying, Elizabeth watched Lucretia join in debates on slavery. She admired the way Lucretia maintained her dignity, even when she was the butt of cruel remarks. And she rejoiced in finding a woman who had enough confidence in herself to hold an opinion when others took sides against her. Lucretia was the first woman she had ever met who believed in the equality of the sexes.

Elizabeth stayed by Lucretia's side throughout their days in London, asking her question after question. Then she attended a lecture Lucretia gave at a London church. It was the first time she had ever heard a woman speak in public to an audience that included men.

On the last day of the convention, Elizabeth and Lucretia walked back to their boardinghouse arm in arm. They talked about calling a women's rights convention as soon as they reached home. Lucretia became involved in other affairs, however, and eight years passed before the convention took place.

Lucretia did start writing to Elizabeth, though. In her letters she suggested books for Elizabeth to read and asked her questions about them. These letters marked the beginning of a forty-year friendship as well as Elizabeth's entrance into "a new world of thought."

Lucretia returned from her trip to a busy home on North Ninth Street in Philadelphia. Her energy was boundless, and she loved having people in. In a letter to her sister she described what she did in just one busy day: "We had a large wash and I hurried to get the ironing [put] away before the people flocked in. Five came before dinner. I prepared mince for forty pies, doing every part myself, even to meat chopping; picked over some lots of apples, stewed a quantity, chopped some more, and made apple pudding."

The doors of the Mott home were open to both the famous and the poor. Besides well-known abolitionists, they also gave dinners for such figures as former President John Quincy Adams, poet Ralph Waldo Emerson, and novelist Charles Dickens. Lucretia paid no mind to Quakers who criticized her for reading Dickens's novels and entertaining him in her home. When the meal was over, Lucretia washed the dishes at the table so that she would not miss a word of the lively after-dinner talk.

Other meals were very, very different. They were suppers served to runaway slaves in the darkened dining room or passed along in a basket to a fugitive being whisked off in a carriage. James was on a committee to help the runaways make their way into nonslave states or Canada.

One man the Motts helped, a slave from Virginia named Henry Brown, escaped to Philadelphia by a clever though risky method: He had himself shipped there in a box by railway express. The Pennsylvania Anti-Slavery Society received a message about a package scheduled to arrive on an early morning train. Sure enough, a crate was delivered to the society's office. When the box could be safely opened, a man stepped out of it, said, "Good morning, gentlemen!", stretched, and took a deep breath of air. He weighed almost two hundred pounds, but he had crammed himself into a box only two feet long, three feet high, and two feet wide. Miraculously, he had survived his twenty-four hour journey. For a long time afterwards Lucretia and James talked about the man who came to be known as "Henry Box Brown."

Though Lucretia was criticized for inviting black people and novelists to her home, there was one visitor who caused even more of a stir. The guest was an actress named Fanny Kemble. Society scorned a woman who appeared on a stage, and tongues wagged and eyebrows rose about the two women's friendship. But they developed a special bond in spite of the gossip.

Fanny had married a Philadelphia man and had spent a year on his large plantation in Georgia, which was worked by slaves. Seeing firsthand the brutality and inhuman treatment the slaves suffered filled her with deep pain. She felt that she could no longer remain the wife of a man who had so little regard for human life. And so she divorced her husband, returned to the North, and wrote a book that described her year on a Southern plantation.

As a result of the divorce, the custody of Fanny's children automatically went to their father. She was not considered to have any rights in the matter. As the law stood, she would not even be allowed to see her children until they reached the age of twenty-one.

Hearing Fanny's story sharpened Lucretia's own feelings about the way women in her society were treated. For a long time she had found that her antislavery efforts were seriously hampered because of the fact that she was a woman. She didn't see how she could get her message across and do any good if she was continually ridiculed or threatened on account of her sex.

All throughout the 1840s Lucretia traveled from state to state to attend meetings and to lecture. The audiences, if not always polite, were at least growing in number. One evening, in the midst of a heavy rainstorm, she spoke in a tent to a crowd of five thousand people!

Lucretia's speeches were described as calm and clear, and her voice was silvery. Nothing would make slavery right, she said over and over again to her audiences. Not the U.S. Constitution, not the argument that it was necessary for the economy, and not biblical passages. "I love the truths of the Bible," Lucretia remarked, "but I never was educated to love the errors of the Bible."

Usually she remained patient with those who attacked her views, but there were times when she found it hard to hold her temper. Once after getting nowhere with a stubborn man, she turned and left the room. "All I have to say to thee in parting," she called to him over her shoulder, "is get thee behind me, Satan!"

Prompted by her Inner Light, she was now speaking out on women's issues. At the Ohio Yearly Meeting of Friends in 1845, she spoke to an entirely female audience, something no woman in the Midwest had ever done. She talked to the women about their right to an equal education, to sue in court, and to keep their own property if they married. At this time such rights were no more than dreams.

The year 1848 marked an important time in the women's rights movement. The first Woman's Rights

Convention was called that summer in Seneca Falls, New York, and Lucretia was one of its organizers.

Three hundred women gathered for the convention, which was held on July 19 and 20. It was still considered bad taste for a woman to lead a meeting, so James Mott filled the role. He then called upon his wife, who gladly stepped forward and delivered an important speech, explaining the purpose of the meeting. Lucretia also put forth one of the resolutions that passed, a belief close to her heart. It called for men and women to work together to secure women's right to take part in professions, trades, and businesses. At a time when very few doors were open to working women, she was looking forward to the end of sex discrimination on the job.

On another issue Lucretia did not look so far into the future. When the convention was being planned, Elizabeth Cady Stanton had brought up the question of voting. "Oh, Lizzie," Lucretia cried, "thou will make us ridiculous! We must go slowly!" Yet a resolution on giving women voting rights passed by a narrow margin.

The convention closed with a speech by Lucretia that was full of faith and courage. Then it was time to sign the Declaration of Sentiments that had been drawn up by the five women who had planned the meeting. As the most respected woman there, Lucretia Mott was asked to put her name first.

Outside of the hall the convention received nothing but bad publicity. People called it nasty names, and newspapers termed it "shocking" and "unnatural." One newspaper ran a headline that read "Woman's Wrong Convention." The news of the meeting was carried to other cities, though, and many women were comforted to learn that others shared their thoughts and feelings.

Soon afterwards, a second meeting was held. This time a woman took charge, although Lucretia and Elizabeth thought this action was "a hazardous experiment."

A main topic at the second convention centered around the question, "Is the female inferior to the male? Is she by nature weaker and less intelligent?" This popular belief was often given as a reason for keeping women out of public life. It was also used to explain why the laws that governed women were made only by men.

Lucretia was the woman chosen to speak on the question. She began by explaining that for centuries women had been held back and denied learning. Because of that, she went on, it caused the women to *appear* to be mentally inferior to men. Yet it cannot be assumed, she said, that women are born with less mental ability than men, or that nothing can be done about their supposedly weak minds.

Then Lucretia took a different approach. Suppose for the sake of argument, she said, it was true that women were born with a smaller brain capacity than men. "Does one man have fewer rights than another because his intellect is inferior?" she asked. "If not, why should a woman?"

Continuing on, Lucretia skillfully built her case against women's inferiority. Her careful approach made it difficult for her opponents to challenge her reasoning.

Taking clues from Lucretia, many women learned to build strong arguments in the way that she did. Then they began conducting conventions in cities all over New York, Ohio, Massachusetts, Pennsylvania, and Indiana.

In 1852 more than two thousand women from eight states and Canada met in Syracuse, New York, for the Third National Woman's Rights Convention. Lucretia was elected its president. Her sister Martha Wright was chosen to be a secretary along with a new member, Susan B. Anthony. Susan, a serious young woman strongly in favor of giving women the right to vote, was to become one of the most important figures of the movement.

While presiding over the meeting in Syracuse, Lucretia was increasingly confronted with religious arguments. "Let your women be silent in the churches; for it is not permitted unto them to speak" was a biblical passage frequently quoted by her opponents. Lucretia knew that responding to these kinds of arguments would only lead to unending debates about the Bible instead of women's rights. Nothing would be gained by answering people who used the Bible as a weapon, and valuable time would be wasted. Wisely, she ruled to keep religion out of the meetings.

Convention after convention was called. Some were peaceful, but some required the use of police to keep order. Few changes were brought about as a result of the work done by Lucretia and her companions, however. The fact remained that women were still ridiculed and were not much better off than before.

Lucretia could not help but be somewhat discouraged by this lack of progress. She even thought that the women's movement belonged to younger leaders, believing that "nobody likes to hear old folks talk," as her mother used to say. Yet in Lucretia's case this saying wasn't true. The invitations for her to speak and pleas for her guidance continued to pour in.

In the hope that his wife would slow down, James urged Lucretia to move to Roadside, a country home outside of Philadelphia. Lucretia loved living there.

Reading in the sunny parlor (which she refused to darken with fashionable but heavy drapes), picking peas from her own garden for dinner, and taking long walks along quiet lanes delighted her.

Yet Lucretia continued to feel that she had a duty to speak out on issues relating to women. In January 1861 she was in Albany, New York, where she first attended a women's rights meeting and then gave a speech to the New York State legislature on divorce. She had just celebrated her sixty-eighth birthday. Perhaps more than she knew, she believed what she had once quipped to her sister Martha: "It takes a Quaker woman to raise her voice."

The Civil War began in April 1861, when Confederate troops opened fire on Fort Sumter. The outbreak of war grieved the Motts who, as Quakers, so deeply believed that it was wrong to fight except with the power of words. They prayed a good deal for the end of the war during the four years that it lasted.

Even though Lucretia was against the war, she followed the news of it closely. She grew to feel that President Lincoln was waiting too long to declare freedom for the slaves and was disappointed with the Emancipation Proclamation. It was not issued until the middle of the war, and it only freed the slaves in Southern states then under Confederate control. Slaves in states that had not left the Union were still legal property.

The war years were full of sorrow for Lucretia. She not only grieved that so many lives were being lost in battle, but she experienced personal suffering as well. After a long illness, her daughter Elizabeth died. Then two years later, James came down with pneumonia, and it brought on the death of her lifelong companion. The only joy she had was in the children and grandchildren who visited and played at Roadside.

But Lucretia did not linger in her grief, and her energies were soon put into working for peace. In 1870 she was elected president of the Pennsylvania Peace Society, an office James had held, and stayed at this post until her death. In addition, she gave her time to charities that aided ill, aged black people and that sent teachers to the South to help former slaves learn to read and write.

And she was always available to the women's movement. Against her doctor's advice, she made a trip to Rochester, New York, for the thirtieth anniversary celebration of the first Woman's Rights Convention. Having reached the age of eighty-four, Lucretia had come to say good-bye. She talked happily about the "bright young women now ready to fill our soon-to-be vacant places. I want to shake hands with them all before I go." Then she left the speaker's platform and moved toward the crowd. Everyone in the audience rose, began clapping, and reached out to touch her hand.

Two years later—on November 11, 1880—she died at Roadside. More than a thousand people followed her plain coffin from her home to the burial grounds.

The National Woman Suffrage Association had a service of its own for Lucretia in the nation's capital. Elizabeth Cady Stanton spoke of her friend as the champion of unpopular causes. In addition, she said that Lucretia's passing "seemed as beautiful and natural" as when the leaves of a "grand old oak" change from their summer to autumn color.

Elizabeth might have added that Lucretia had also stood like a grand old oak during the early years of the women's movement. She had quietly braved the storms of protest that arose when women began to seek respect and equality. And it was this steadfastness as much as anything she did or said that inspired other women to take up the cause.

A LOUD AND PLEADING VOICE

SOJOURNER TRUTH: A slave for thirty years, she was the first black woman to become an abolitionist lecturer. She also campaigned for women's rights, worked to end segregated streetcars, and petitioned that ex-slaves be given land for resettlement.

The tall nine-year-old girl called Belle stood clutching the rough flax strands of her "slave cloth" dress. Her little brother Peter was close by her in the front yard of the master's house. But their parents were held back at the gate, weeping.

Suddenly Belle found herself being shoved up onto a wooden auction block. She could not fully understand what was happening because the English used by the auctioneer made no sense to her. She spoke only Low Dutch, the language of her former owner, one of a number of Dutch settlers living in Ulster County, New York. All she knew was that since the death of her master, Charles Hardenbergh, there had been news of a sale. Now it was finally taking place. His "slaves, horses, and other cattle" were being sold to the highest bidder.

Everything began to happen so fast that it made Belle's head spin. First the auctioneer shouted, "Going, going, gone!" Then he slammed his hammer on a table. And the next thing Belle knew, she was being pulled across the grass towards the gate by a stranger.

At the gate, her parents reached out to touch her as she passed, and her father whispered, "I'll be by to see you Belle. Don't you worry!" But the stranger had no time for them. He was eager to be on his way home with his "bargains."

Soon Belle was stumbling barefooted along the dusty road that led away from Kingston, New York. She was on her way to the nearby town of Twaalfskill, the home of her new owner, a storekeeper named John Neely. Along with a flock of sheep, she had been sold to him for one hundred dollars.

As she walked, Belle remembered the words her mother had often spoken in their cold, dark slave quarters. They were the same words of advice she had given to all her children, who were eventually sold away from her. She begged them never to lie or steal and always to obey their white masters. Years later when Belle told a friend her life's story, she still remembered her mother talking about a "God who hears and sees you. When you are beaten or fall into any trouble, you must ask help of Him and He will always hear and help you."

Belle tried to remember some other comforting words her mother had said, but her thoughts were all jumbled. In fact, only one thing seemed to be clear: She was being taken away from everyone and everything she had ever known.

This was not the first time that Belle would be sold.

Over the years she would become the property of four different owners. Yet despite the hardships she endured, Belle was certain that God was always with her. Indeed, she was so certain that in midlife she changed her name to Sojourner Truth and set out to speak for Him. Until she was eighty-two, she traveled from state to state, crying out against the cruelty of slavery, campaigning for women's rights, and counseling her people.

Although she never learned to read and write, Belle was a powerful speaker for both these causes. Her quick wit and straightforward approach appealed to people. In addition, it was hard to ignore her. She stood six-feet tall, wrapped her head in a white turban, wore a plain gray dress, and spoke in a deep, throaty voice. But most of all, people could believe what she said, for she had personally been wrongly and unjustly treated.

Belle was a slave for about thirty years. For nine of them she belonged to the Hardenbergh family, Dutch landowners who lived about eighty miles up the Hudson River from New York City. In fact, she was born on Colonel Johannes Hardenbergh's estate, probably in 1797. The exact date is unknown, since no one then thought it was important to record a slave's birth. No one thought slaves needed a family name either, and so she was simply named Isabella. The other slaves on the estate shortened it to Belle.

It was unfortunate for Belle that she had not been born two years later than she was. For in 1799 the New York State legislature voted to "free" slaves born after July 4 of that year. They were not to grow up in freedom, though, because the law said that female slaves must work without pay until the age of twenty-five, and males until the age of twenty-eight.

Belle's mother, named Elizabeth, was called Mau-mau Bett. Her father, chosen by Colonel Hardenbergh to raise children with Mau-mau, was named James Baumfree. He was a much older slave than Mau-mau, and she was his third wife. The other two had been sold away from him. Belle and her brother Peter were the last of the thirteen children born to Baumfree and Mau-mau. Some of their children had died, while the rest had been sold to other slaveholders.

Colonel Hardenbergh died when Belle was a baby, and his big farm went to his son Charles. Charles built a new home for himself, but provided only a dark, damp cellar in it for his slaves. They were expected to sleep there on piles of straw thrown over broad floor boards that had been loosely set over slushy, muddy ground.

This cellar was the place where Belle was brought up, where she was cradled on winter nights when it was too dark to work. Here Mau-mau told her about God and the stars in His sky, taught her the Lord's Prayer in Dutch, and sang her songs from Africa.

On the same morning that Belle and Peter were sold, the Hardenbergh heirs were faced with a decision. What were they to do with Belle's father? Old, twisted with rheumatism, and half blind, Baumfree was not considered useful anymore. No one would pay a penny for him. Yet the law said that he couldn't be set free unless the family was willing to support him. After discussing the problem, the heirs decided to free both Baumfree and Mau-mau. That way she could take care of her husband, and the Hardenberghs wouldn't be responsible for either of them.

Freedom was something that slaves only dared dream about. But it was hardly as joyful as Belle's parents had imagined. How could it be, when Baumfree was ill and helpless, when neither of them could earn a living, and when their last two children had been torn from their arms?

The new master's house certainly gave no comfort to Belle, who arrived at it shaking with fright. John Neely hadn't seemed too harsh, but his wife lashed out at her in a shrill, angry voice from the first moment on. Belle truly wanted to please her new owners and to prove herself a good worker. Yet because she spoke only Dutch, she couldn't understand the orders Mistress Neely snapped at her in English. The harder Belle tried to understand those strange words and obey, the louder the mistress shouted at her, and the more often she was punished.

In time the woman complained so much about her young slave that the master began to whip Belle, too. Maybe he had grown angry with his bitter wife or with his failing business at the store. Whatever the reason, Belle never knew what she had done wrong to deserve most of her punishments.

Moments to herself were rare, but when Belle could find time, she slipped away to a field near a row of birch trees. Here she would talk to God in a loud and pleading voice. Mau-mau had promised that He would listen, and so for a long time she asked Him to turn her master and mistress into good folk.

But that winter, an especially bitter one, Belle gave up on that particular prayer because it seemed to have gone unanswered. Despite her pleas to God, the Neely's hadn't changed. She still had nothing to wear but the shabby garment she had arrived in, along with a hand-me-down shawl and a pair of broken shoes. This meant that she nearly froze every time she went outside to tend the cows and sheep or carry firewood. And Mau-mau was no longer around to hold her close and warm her inside and out.

Moreover, that winter she was given the worst beating she had ever remembered receiving. She didn't know what she had done, but one day her master ordered her out to the barn, tied her hands, and beat her fiercely with a bundle of wooden rods. Afterwards, lying in pain on the barn floor, she tried hard to talk to God. "Oh, God," she murmured, "you know how much I am in distress, for I have told you again and again." But He just didn't seem to hear.

Although her prayer went unanswered, Belle did not give up her faith. The next year her patience was rewarded when she was paid a surprise visit by Baumfree. He could not stay long, but the few minutes he shared with his daughter were filled with deep love and concern.

Belle learned that Mau-mau was well and that there was not much news of her brother Peter. Then Baumfree asked about Belle's life. Not wanting him to worry, she tried to tell him that she was well and happy. But as he made ready to go, she could no longer hold in her pain and anguish. Showing him the scars from her recent beating, she broke down and burst into tears, begging him to find her a new master. Shocked and angry, he held her tightly and promised to do what he could. Then he sadly turned away and slowly began walking toward a crossing, where he would catch a ride back home.

A few months later Belle's prayer that Baumfree would find her better owners was answered. Hearing a knock at the door one day, she opened it and saw a gentle-looking man who greeted her in Dutch. Smiling, he asked Belle if she would like to live with his family. She knew then that he would be her new master. He had already paid John Neely $105 for her.

The kindly Dutchman was Martin Schryver, a fisherman, innkeeper, and farmer. Along with his wife and sons, he lived near Kingston, about half a mile up the road from Rondout Creek. Belle was well treated during the year and a half she spent with this warm-hearted family. She remembered being "expected to carry fish, to hoe corn, to bring roots and herbs from the woods for beers, [and to] go to the Strand for a gallon of molasses or liquor as the case might be."

The Schryvers gave her plenty of time to "browse around," as she put it. In the summer she would sit on a pier on the shore of the Hudson River and watch the boats drift by. In the winter when the river froze, she tied smooth beef bones to her feet and skated. She prayed less and sang more, and the songs she made up pleased her most of all.

During her time with the Schryvers, Belle turned thirteen and grew to be six-feet tall, her full adult height. She also began wearing a bandanna over her head, which was a sign of womanhood among her people.

This pleasant time was all too short. One day a customer in Martin Schryver's tavern offered $300 for Belle. The family didn't want to lose such an obedient girl, but they decided that they needed the money, and Belle was sold once again. Her new master, John Dumont, owned ten slaves and a big farm in New Paltz, New York, fifteen miles from Kingston.

Belle became one of Dumont's house slaves and was his property for seventeen years. She worked in the kitchen alongside an older girl named Kate, a white orphan from the county poorhouse. Master Dumont praised Belle's work, but Mistress Dumont was never satisfied with it. In part, this was because Kate played tricks in order to get Belle into trouble.

One of Belle's early morning jobs was to put out boiled potatoes for the family. One morning they were found dirty, and Belle was warned to be more careful. She did her best to obey, but for three successive mornings the potatoes were no cleaner. Master Dumont grew more and more angry and harshly scolded Belle each day, despite her tearful pleas that she was innocent. Finally, Dumont's daughter Gertrude proved that Belle was telling the truth. She showed her father that Kate had been sweeping up ashes from the hearth so that they would land on the boiling potatoes.

Belle never received an apology, however, and she continued to be frightened of displeasing her master. To avoid punishment she worked harder and longer, until she often fell asleep standing against a wall. Yet her efforts only created more problems. Dumont was happy with her work, and she became his favorite slave. But the other slaves began to criticize her. They said that by working so hard she made them look bad by comparison. They called her "white man's pet" and stopped talking to her. Cut off from her own people, she felt lonelier than ever.

As a result of her loneliness, Belle began to pray again frequently. She was so troubled and confused, though, that she came to believe that Master Dumont was a "Mighty Being" like God. She thought that her master knew all her thoughts and feelings, and feared that she was not being good enough for him. This fear even led her to confess what she considered to be her sins to Dumont. So great was his influence that for a long time she believed that slavery was "right and honorable."

Belle's loneliness was complete when she learned that Mau-mau had died and that Baumfree was barely alive. Allowed to attend her mother's funeral, Belle tried to tell her father that she would soon be able to come and care for him. He was too overcome with grief to do anything but cry, however.

Belle saw her father only a few more times after the funeral. At their last meeting, she told him that in ten years she would be free.

"But my child, I cannot live that long," he said.

"Oh, do, daddy, do live!" she cried, "and I will take such good care of you."

Sadly, Baumfree did die of cold and starvation a few years later.

Not long before her father's death, Master Dumont chose one of his male slaves as a mate for Belle. He had decided that at seventeen she was old enough to have children. All the children born to her would be his property because the law said that the offspring of a female slave always belonged to her master.

Belle was not legally married to Tom, the man Dumont had selected to be her husband. Stooped and haggard-looking, he was years older than she was and had been married twice before. Apparently, his other wives had been sold away from him, just as had happened to Baumfree. When his second wife was sold, Tom ran off to search for her. He had managed to get many miles from Dumont's farm before slavehunters tracked him down. Brutally whipped on his return, he never again tried to escape.

Between 1815 and 1825, Belle and Tom had five children—Diana, Peter, Elizabeth, Hannah, and Sophia. Little else is known about their life together, however, except that Belle left him long before she gained her freedom.

During the years Belle spent on Dumont's farm, New Yorkers heatedly debated whether to abolish slavery. Some of them wanted all slaves to be freed, or emancipated, immediately. Others felt that the state legislature had gone far enough in passing the law of 1799 that freed slave children born after July 4 of that year—females at age twenty-five and males at twenty-eight.

Finally, though, the eventual emancipation of all the slaves in the state was guaranteed. In 1817 legislators voted to free slaves born *before* July 4, 1799. There was a catch, however. The law stated that these slaves would not be freed until July 4, 1827. They had to wait ten more long years!

At first Belle did not think ten more years would be too long to wait. She was thrilled with the idea that she would at last be free. But the years passed slowly, and near the end of the decade, everything suddenly appeared bleak again.

Without warning, Master Dumont suddenly sold Belle's four-year old son Peter to a doctor named Solomon Gedney. Belle was heartbroken, but she had no power to stop him. For although her son had been born "free," Dumont could sell his right to Peter's services until the boy was twenty-eight.

Shortly after Peter was sent away, another series of events made Belle realize that Master Dumont was not a good and "Mighty Being" after all. First, Dumont promised that he would free Belle and Tom one year early if she worked extra hard for him. She did just as he asked, continuing to labor even when she cut her hand to the bone with a scythe blade. But as the date of her freedom approached, the master said nothing about it. Then when Belle reminded him of the promise, he changed his mind. He told her that the accident had slowed down her work. And he said that because the wheat crop had been poor that year, he could not afford to let her go.

Belle was more deeply wounded by his words than by the scythe. She later told a friend that "slave holders are terrible for promising you this or that, . . . and when the time of fulfillment comes, and one claims the promise, they recollect nothing." She knew that she had kept her end of the bargain, though, and she was determined to have her freedom. And so early on a summer morning in 1826, she disobeyed a master for the first time in her life. Leaving her older daughters in the care of Dumont's other slaves, she gathered a few belongings, picked up baby Sophia, and walked away from the farm.

With the help of a kindly man named Levi Rowe, Belle found a new place to earn her keep. She and Sophia were taken in by the Van Wageners, a Quaker family who lived near New Paltz. They did not believe in slavery, but they bought her services from Dumont so that she and her child would not have to return to him.

Belle was well treated by the Van Wageners, but their quiet, patterned lives were not suited to her active mind and spirit. More and more she longed to return to Dumont's farm, where life was hard but bustling. Finally, she decided to go back to her old master, but a powerful religious experience changed her plans.

According to the story she told years later, Belle

claimed that a spiritual presence had stopped her from leaving the Van Wageners. Then when she realized that she had fully intended to return to slavery, she "felt so wicked, . . . as if God would surely burn [her] up." In despair she cried out, "Oh somebody, somebody stand between God and me." When she did, she believed that Jesus Christ revealed himself to her. His appearance filled her with love for all creatures, and he became the moving force in her life.

As a result of this experience, Belle stayed on with the Van Wagners. When she legally gained her freedom on July 4, 1827, they began paying her a small wage. It was only enough to support her and Sophia, however. Her other three daughters stayed at Dumont's farm, while her husband Tom worked at odd jobs and found shelter wherever he could.

Belle thought her son Peter was still living with Doctor Gedney. Then she learned that he had sold the little boy to his brother-in-law in Alabama. This news was terrifying. If Peter had been sent to the South, where slavery was still thriving, he would never be free.

At first Belle didn't know what to do. But with the help of some friendly Quakers, she discovered that in New York slaves could not be sold for transportation out of the state. Furthermore, Peter was already legally free, since he had been born after July 4, 1799.

After learning these things, Belle no longer felt powerless. Even though she was completely inexperienced in the ways of the white people's world, she was determined to get her son back. Years later she recalled, "I felt so tall within—I felt as if the power of a nation was with me."

Following the instructions of a kindly Quaker, Belle

appeared before the Grand Jury in Kingston to tell her story. It ordered Solomon Gedney to bring Peter back to the state of New York. Faced with the possibility of a long prison term or a large fine, Gedney traveled to Alabama to get the boy. Belle was then told by her lawyer that she would have to wait several months for the court to hand Peter over to her. Not wanting to wait that long, she found another lawyer. He told her that she could have the boy the next day for five dollars. This was the fee a constable would charge to get her son from Gedney. Belle got more than enough money, and the lawyer kept his promise. Scarred from beatings and frightened out of his wits, Peter was reunited with his mother in a judge's chamber. Belle had taken white men to court and had come away in triumph!

Belle's concern for Peter brought her to New York City in 1829. Miss Geer, a teacher Belle had met, told her that he could be sent to trade school there and learn to be a sailor. She also said that Belle would have no trouble finding a well-paying job. And so Belle decided to put little Sophia in her older sisters' care at the Dumonts' farm and leave Ulster County. Tom, whom she did not see before she left, was now living in the county poorhouse. Records indicate that he later died there.

Miss Geer helped Peter start school and found a family who hired Belle to work as a maid. She also took Belle out into the streets of New York City to preach with a group of devout women who were bringing the Word of God to the poor.

In the slums of a place known as Five Points, Belle saw homeless women—beggars and prostitutes—whose lives were as hopeless as those bound in slavery. Most of them ignored her as she walked through the halls of the tenement buildings. They huddled in the dark corners of their filthy rooms, too sick and dazed to come to Miss Geer's street meetings. A few longed for a miracle and desperately clutched at the tall, stately black woman who talked so movingly of what God had done for her. Belle knew that she was no miracle worker, though, and she looked for a more practical way to help people.

Her next try at doing the Lord's work met with somewhat more success. At the Magdalene Asylum for homeless girls, she agreed to teach domestic skills every Sunday. She thought that training the girls as servants might spare them the hopelessness of Five Points.

One Sunday she met a man at the asylum who claimed he had been appointed to establish God's kingdom on earth. Easily swayed, Belle joined him in a religious community outside of the city. In time she realized that there was no peace and love in the little cult. Instead, there was a lack of cooperation, and hours filled with argument. Besides, as the only black member, she was doing most of the kingdom's work—housework!

The cult broke up after Matthias, the leader, was charged with murdering another member. Belle was also accused of taking part in the crime, but she cleared herself in court. She also sued her accusers for slander, claiming they had damaged her good name. She easily won this suit and was even awarded some money.

During the time that Belle had spent in the cult, Peter had become a troublesome young man. He lied, cheated, quit school, and spent his days with hoodlums. Hoping that life at sea might change his ways, Belle arranged for him to work aboard a whaling ship. She received a handful of letters from him, but he later disappeared, and she never heard from him again.

For nine years Belle worked for a family in New York City, all the while becoming closer to God. Finally one day in 1843 she received a message from Him. He wanted her to leave the city and go east. It was a call so clear and true that she felt she must follow it. She tucked a few coins in her pocket and quit her job the very next day. Then she headed east towards Long Island on foot.

As she walked along a sandy road, God gave her a new first name—Sojourner, or traveler. Her mission was "to travel up and down the land, showing the people their sins, and being a sign to them." She then decided to take one of God's titles, Truth, for her last name. And so at the age of forty-six, Isabella Van Wagener became Sojourner Truth.

Sleeping in sheds or under the stars when she was refused lodging, Sojourner chanced upon a camp meeting in Long Island. Thousands of families had come to this meeting to spend several days hearing speakers and sharing their religious beliefs. They were camping out in wagons and tents. Before the meeting was over, Sojourner asked if she could speak.

With great dignity, she rose above the crowd. Then she began to talk about human sin and suffering in her deep, powerful voice. Possessed with an astounding memory, she quoted long passages from the Bible that had only been read to her a few times. She also sang to the crowd. Some songs were hymns she had heard, while others were songs she had made up, such as this one:

We are going home; we soon shall be
Where the sky is clear, and the soil is free;
Where the victor's song floats over the plains,
And the seraph's anthem blends with the strains.

During that camp meeting, Sojourner discovered that she held a command over her listeners. Her striking appearance, powerful voice, and original way of speaking seemed to cast a spell over people. One witness at a later speech said that Sojourner left many in the audience with "streaming eyes, and hearts beating with gratitude."

More religious meetings followed in New York, and then in Connecticut and Massachusetts. When Sojourner grew weary, friends suggested that she settle for a while at the Northampton Association of Education and Industry in Florence, Massachusetts. It was a community of people of all religions, races, and backgrounds. Equality for all was their common belief and purpose. Many of the association's members had risked their lives to help slaves escape into free states by way of a secret system called the Underground Railroad.

The community's members lived and worked in an old, abandoned factory, raising silkworms and weaving cloth from the silk. Grim as their surroundings were, they remained a people full of sunshine and passion. Sojourner joined them as chief laundress.

While living in the community, Sojourner met several important abolitionist leaders. Among them were William Lloyd Garrison and Frederick Douglass. Garrison was the publisher of the famous antislavery newspaper, *The Liberator*. Douglass was a young man who had escaped from slavery in 1840 and had taught himself to read and write. He was to become a great black leader and a speaker for women's rights. At the time Sojourner met him, however, he had just begun to speak out on abolition.

Sojourner belonged to the Northampton Association for three years. At that point the silkworm business failed, and the group was forced to disband. Once again Sojourner found herself working in people's homes, but she kept the friendship of many community members.

One of these friends, Olive Gilbert, saw the importance of recording Sojourner's life story in a book. Olive wanted to show people that slavery had been just as cruel and unjust in the North as it now was in the South. And she believed that Sojourner's story would gain support for the abolitionist movement.

Once Sojourner agreed to tell her story, Olive took down her words. In addition, she talked to many of Sojourner's friends and acquaintances. Then she put all of the information together and wrote her book, which was printed in Boston in 1850. It was entitled the *Narrative of Sojourner Truth, A Northern Slave.*

Whenever Sojourner spoke or attended meetings, she put her book on sale. Fortunately, it sold well, for she needed the money it brought in to pay for a house a friend had built for her in Northampton. Later she also sold copies of her songs and her photograph, using this money to meet her traveling expenses.

The year the *Narrative* was printed, Congress passed legislation which set back the campaign against slavery. Known as the Fugitive Slave Law, it provided that runaway slaves living in free states must be returned to their masters. Before this, the runaways were usually safe if they made it to a free state. The law also stated that anyone caught helping a runaway was subject to a large fine.

Outraged at what they saw as the injustice of this law, abolitionists stepped up their work. They set up more meetings and called for more speakers. Sojourner and her friends went on a lengthy lecture tour. Sometimes they were well received, but they often had to deal with violent mobs, knife and pistol-wielding citizens, or hecklers.

One man approached Sojourner and said, "Old woman, do you think your talk about slavery does any good? Do you suppose people care what you say? Why I don't care any more for your talk than I do for the bite of a flea."

"Perhaps not," answered Sojourner," but the Lord willing, I'll keep you scratchin'!"

Antislavery crusaders were not the only reformers who faced strong opposition. People who became involved in the women's rights movement were also subjected to ridicule and violence. If a woman dared to give a public lecture, her behavior was labeled improper and even immoral. Often, riots broke out at a lecture, and rocks and eggs were hurled at speakers. And the protesters against the movement were not only men. Throngs of women also opposed the idea that females should have the right to vote, to attend school, to receive equal pay for equal work, and to own property.

Many of the abolitionists and the people working for women's rights found a common bond in one another's crusades. Not all abolitionists wanted to combine them, however. They were afraid that asking for too much social change at once would hamper the antislavery effort. As a result, the abolitionists split into two factions. One group concentrated on freeing the slaves. The other campaigned for the freedom of both blacks and women.

Sojourner met many of the people who championed both causes while she was living in the Northampton community. After listening to what they said, she, too, began to speak for the rights of both blacks and women. In October of 1850 she went to the first National Woman's Rights Convention in Worcester, Massachusetts, as a delegate from that state. She heard speeches by her old friends William Lloyd Garrison and Frederick Douglass, and her new acquaintances Lucretia Mott and Lucy Stone.

After Sojourner heard many fiery addresses, someone read her a statement printed in a newspaper. It said, "Woman's offices are those of wife, mother, daughter, sister, friend—Good God, can they not be content with these?" She could not help but marvel at the question, since she had never been given a chance to fulfill any of those roles. Indeed, for thirty years she had been nothing but a slave, and now as a free woman she had fewer rights than a free man!

The convention concluded by adopting the motto, "Equality before the law without distinction of sex or color." Afterwards, Sojourner began to stress this idea in the talks she gave. In 1851 she attended another women's rights convention in Akron, Ohio. Ohio was a free state, but its citizens were mixed in their feelings about slavery. Therefore, when Sojourner entered the meeting hall, many people were shocked to see the graying, six-foot black woman.

Some women were afraid to allow her to speak. They had already received enough bad publicity, and they didn't want any more. But convention leader Frances Gage called Sojourner forward. Gage later wrote that Sojourner "moved slowly and solemnly to the front, laid her old bonnet at her feet and turned her great speaking eyes to me."

Then Sojourner looked at the audience and said, "That man over there says that women need to be helped into carriages, and lifted over ditches, and to have the best place everywhere. Nobody ever helps me into carriages, or over mud puddles, or gives me any best place, and aren't I a woman? Look at me! Look at my arm! I have plowed, and planted, and gathered into barns, and no man could head me—and aren't I a woman? I could work as much and eat as much as a man (when I could get it), and bear the lash as well—and aren't I a woman?"

The rest of Sojourner's speech was equally dramatic and moving. Her stirring words silenced the strongest opponents of womens' rights in the audience. "I have never in my life seen anything like the magical influence that subdued the mobbish spirit of the day," Frances Gage said. "Hundreds rushed up to shake hands with her, and congratulate the glorious old mother, and bid her God-speed on her mission."

After an exhaustive tour throughout Ohio, Sojourner took her lectures into other midwestern states. Many of the settlers in this region were still undecided about slavery, and the issue was being hotly debated. People who favored slavery often tried to disrupt speeches by abolitionists like Sojourner.

On one occasion a man interrupted her as she began to speak. Because of her height, strength, and deep voice, he accused her—of all things—of being a man in disguise. He even demanded that she let some of the women in the audience see her breasts! To answer him and all the other doubters in the crowd, Sojourner opened her blouse and said, "It is not my shame but yours that I do this."

As people's feelings about slavery grew stronger,

uprisings and rebellions over it became more frequent. In 1856 settlers from Missouri and Kansas fought with each other about the issue. On October 16, 1859, John Brown, a fiery abolitionist, tried to seize guns stored in the federal arsenal at Harper's Ferry, Virginia, planning to distribute them to slaves. Finally, eleven southern states seceded, or withdrew, from the Union, and in April 1861 the Civil War began.

By that time Sojourner had settled in Battle Creek, Michigan, where her daughters Elizabeth and Hannah, now married, were living. She remained there throughout much of the war, part of the time battling against illness.

On January 1, 1863, President Abraham Lincoln issued the Emancipation Proclamation. It declared that all the slaves living in Southern states under Confederate control were "forever free." It did not include slaves in the border states of Delaware, Kentucky, Maryland, and Missouri. Not until the Thirteenth Amendment to the Constitution was made in December of 1865 were all the slaves freed.

As a result of the proclamation, thousands of slaves ran away from their masters. In fact, by the end of the war more than half a million slaves had fled to freedom behind Northern lines. By enlisting in the Union Army or Navy, or serving the armed forces as laborers, these former slaves helped the North to win the war.

About five months after the proclamation was issued, Sojourner set out for Washington, D.C., to meet President Lincoln. She wanted to thank him for what he had done and to learn where she might be most useful in helping her people. When they finally met she told Lincoln that she thought he was America's greatest president. The other men who had led the country "may have been good to others," she said, "but they neglected to do anything for my race."

Despite her joy in seeing Lincoln, Sojourner grieved when she saw how little freedom had changed the daily lives of the blacks in the North. Thousands of them lived in tents and shacks. Unable to read or write, they couldn't find jobs. And they were generally not treated with courtesy or respect by white people. In many Northern cities, for example, blacks could not ride in the same streetcars with whites.

One time Sojourner tried to ride a whites-only car in Washington, D.C. A conductor told her to leave, and when she refused, he threw her off. Sojourner took the man to court, charging that he had dislocated her shoulder. A judge agreed, and the conductor lost his job. The victory pleased Sojourner as much as when she had won back her son Peter in court years before.

For a time Sojourner worked for a relief association, counseling the freed slaves and distributing clothes. Yet that was not enough for her. She also tried to get the government to see that blacks needed land in order to earn a living. Plenty of unused land was available in the abandoned rice plantations of South Carolina and in the rolling plains of Kansas. But the government turned a deaf ear to her pleas.

Sojourner also worked to get blacks and women the right to vote. But as she grew older, she was forced to cut down on her travels. Nevertheless, even at the age of eighty-one she was still giving speeches in Michigan, and she traveled to Rochester, New York, to attend the thirtieth anniversary meeting of the first Woman's Rights Convention.

Gradually, though, Sojourner's health declined. Plagued by ulcers on her legs, which caused her great pain, she took to her bed. When it was clear that she would not recover, many of her friends came to visit her. They were sorrowful, but she was at peace. Shortly before her death she said, "I'm not going to die honey; I'm going home like a shooting star."

Sojourner died in Battle Creek on November 26, 1883, at the age of eighty-six. For forty years she had done what she believed was the work of the Lord. This work was often difficult and dangerous, but it won her much respect and admiration. Indeed, few people have made a greater contribution to the struggle for justice and human rights than Sojourner Truth.

A QUEEN AMONG WOMEN

ELIZABETH CADY STANTON: She helped organize the first Woman's Rights Convention, became the first woman to run for Congress, and was the first president of the National Woman Suffrage Association.

In all her eleven years, Elizabeth Cady had never experienced such sadness. After a long illness, her older brother Eleazer had just died and now lay in a darkened room of her family's house. Seated beside his body was her father, torn by grief and praying for comfort and support. Elizabeth knew how much he had loved his only son. She knew how he had planned to take him into his law practice.

Slowly Elizabeth approached her father. She wanted to reach out to him, to let him know how much she too cared.

For a moment he paid no attention to her. Then at last he put his arm around her, sighed deeply, and said, "Oh my daughter, I wish you were a boy."

"I will try to be all my brother was," she cried out in response.

From that moment on Elizabeth made up her mind to strive to take Eleazer's place in the family. What was most important in a boy's life? she asked herself. Courage and education, she decided. She would begin by studying Greek and learning to ride a horse.

Elizabeth Cady hurried to her pastor and friend, the Reverend Simon Hosack. When she asked him to be her tutor, he replied that he would be delighted to teach her, and they began at once.

Despite the solemn weeks of mourning that followed her brother's death, Elizabeth progressed rapidly in her lessons. As she did, she waited day after day for her father to say, "Well, a girl is as good as a boy, after all." But he said no such thing.

When the Reverend Hosack came to call, Elizabeth urged him to tell her father how capable she was. Yet even after he did so, her father still did not see her as the equal of the son he had lost. Deeply hurt, tears filled her eyes, and she wanted to cry. But she held back and decided to work even harder to please Mr. Cady. She was determined to prove herself her brother's equal, no matter how much time and effort it took.

As it turned out, Elizabeth spent a half century proving herself the equal of any man and working to improve the place of women in society. Early in her crusade she decided that the best way to better women's lives was to change the many laws that denied them the same rights as men. And in her view the best way to change those laws was by persuading men to give women the suffrage, or right to vote. Working for this right became her primary goal.

In organizing and leading the country's first women's rights conventions, Elizabeth became known as the "mother of the woman's suffrage movement." She was also the mother of seven children, whom she raised with the help of servants. At times she was set back in her work because the help was not adequate or the children became ill. But she tried not to let household problems interfere with her efforts too much.

She traveled, gave hundreds of speeches, headed conventions, helped edit a newspaper, cofounded a national women's suffrage organization, contributed to newspapers and magazines, and wrote books. Her autobiography—*Eighty Years and More*—shows that she wrote as beautifully as she spoke.

Elizabeth's work was all done against the tide of the times in which she lived. Almost every one of her ideas, words, and actions was criticized or ridiculed by the outside world. One college president said that women's rights were "too ridiculous to appear credible." A spokesman for the church announced that "we do not believe women are fit to have their own heads." Other people spoke of "the feeble female brain."

Answering these criticisms required Elizabeth to be brave and cool-headed. And in time the *Philadelphia Press* came to realize that she had a "rare talent for affairs, management, and mastership."

When Elizabeth's father had wished that she was a boy, he had not meant to be unkind or to hurt her. For even though Judge Daniel Cady was a cold and stern man, he cared deeply for his wife and five daughters. But during the nineteenth century most people thought that girls were less important than boys. Boys were expected to grow up and make a name for themselves in business, politics, or a profession like law. Girls were only expected to become wives and mothers. Judge Cady had always hoped that his son Eleazer would be an outstanding lawyer. When the young man died, the judge felt he had no one left to be proud of. To him Elizabeth would always be just a girl.

This, then, was the world into which Elizabeth Cady was born on November 12, 1815. Judge Cady was the master of his family, which included Elizabeth's mother Margaret, her brother Eleazer, and her sisters Tryphena, Harriet, Madge, and Kate. Because Mrs. Cady was often ill, she and Elizabeth did not have a close relationship.

Rosy-cheeked Elizabeth treasured the merry times she spent playing in the rooms of the Cady's large house in Johnstown, New York, that the children were forbidden to enter. Sometimes they managed to sneak into the garret and nibble on the hickory nuts and maple sugar that were stored there. Other times they tiptoed into the cellar amidst the cider, butter, and barrels of apples, and played games like blindman's bluff. Often they were joined there by Peter Teabout, the family's black servant. He was a lad who played the violin, told exciting stories, and made wonderful flapjacks. Peter had a friend stand guard at the cellar door, lest Judge Cady should find them all out.

Despite these fun times, Elizabeth didn't always enjoy her childhood. She did not like being forced to behave properly and be ladylike at all times. In particular, she hated the red flannel dresses with starched neck ruffles that she and her sisters had to wear to all outings for many years. On Sundays the sisters also had to wear red hoods, red stockings, and red mittens. And if the girls complained, their Scottish nurse Mary Dunn was instructed to slap or scold them. In her autobiography Elizabeth recalled that words could not express her dislike for the red outfits.

Elizabeth's religious upbringing created an even more disturbing problem. Her parents taught her to fear God, to believe in the Bible, and to pray that she would go to heaven after death. In their view only a small number of people had been chosen by God to live in heaven. Most people, they thought, would spend the afterlife in a fiery hell as a punishment for sin.

Elizabeth found these beliefs very frightening. She could believe in God and the Bible, but religion seemed to be nothing but gloomy lessons and constant talk of punishment for one's sins. She later wrote that such teachings caused her to "suffer endless fears" during her childhood and teenage years.

Once she tried to express those fears and worries to her nurse. She had been staring out of the nursery window when she wondered out loud why everything she liked to do was called a sin. She wanted to know if life was nothing but "thou shalt not's." Nurse Mary was shocked at these questions. She could only scold the child and remind her how important it was to concentrate on obedience and humility.

Elizabeth gained a little freedom when she and her sisters were enrolled in the Johnstown Academy. There they met the daughters of the county sheriff and a hotel keeper. Suddenly the county jailhouse and the hotel were exciting places of adventure for the girls. At the jailhouse they watched trials and sneaked candy and cakes to the prisoners. At the hotel they helped wait on tables.

In the dining room of the hotel Elizabeth once overheard two lawyers discussing a case, and she could not help but interrupt and add an opinion of her own. One of the men told her she ought to mind her business and asked to be served a glass of water at once.

"I am not a servant," she answered boldly. "I am here for fun!"

Giving an opinion about a case of law came very naturally to Elizabeth. She was often sent to her father's law office as a punishment for misbehavior. There she spent many hours reading his law books and listening to his clients discuss their problems with him.

Many of the people who came to her father's office were women. Some of them complained that they had been robbed of their inheritances. Others were widows who claimed that they had lost their personal property to a selfish son or stepson. A number of them sobbed that they had been beaten by a drunken husband. Judge Cady was forced to turn most of these women away. As the laws then stood, men had almost complete control over a woman's life and property.

For a long time Elizabeth could not understand why these laws could not be changed. After all, as her father had shown her, they were only words written down in big, heavy books. All that someone needed to do, she decided, was to take a scissors and cut out the pages with the laws that were unfair to women.

Luckily, Judge Cady stopped his daughter before she damaged his law books. He explained that cutting out a page would not change anything. The laws were made by the state legislature, he told her, and they were printed in all the law books throughout New York. Then he suggested that perhaps she could work to make better laws for women when she grew up. Little did he imagine that one day Elizabeth would in fact influence the New York legislature to give women more legal rights.

Elizabeth was already proving that women were not inferior to men. At Johnstown Academy she was the only girl in a class of boys, but she was one of the best students. One year she took second prize in the school's Greek language competition.

Certain that this award would finally win her father's approval, she raced home to show it to him. Bounding breathlessly into his office, she waved the prize before him and said, "There, I got it!" He looked at the Greek Testament, asked her a few questions about the class, and seemed pleased. But she still had not taken Eleazer's place for him. For once again he sighed deeply and said, "You should have been a boy." Heartbroken, Elizabeth fought back her tears. Later she wrote that "my joy was turned to sadness."

When Elizabeth turned sixteen, she wanted to enroll at Union College in Schenectady, New York, along with the boys in her class. But she could not join them because at that time no college in the nation admitted women. Instead, she continued her education at the Troy Female Seminary, a fashionable girl's boarding school in Troy, New York, run by Mrs. Emma Willard. Elizabeth later criticized the school for not having a strong academic program, but she found her classmates friendly and enjoyed learning French, music, and dancing.

Elizabeth did not leave Mrs. Willard's seminary happily, though. While she was there she attended a series of revival meetings that brought back her childhood fears and feelings of despair about the afterlife.

Listening to sermons by the famous preacher Charles Grandison Finney made her feel like a "miserable, helpless, forsaken worm." His descriptions of the devil, hell, and everlasting punishment were so vivid that she sometimes imagined she was "falling into the bottomless pit." As a result of dwelling on the idea of sin, she soon became very depressed and even thought that she might be going insane.

Fortunately, her parents saw that her health was threatened and they brought her home. Then her father, her oldest sister Tryphena, and Tryphena's new husband Edward Bayard took her on a vacation to Niagara Falls. Comforted and relaxed, she rested and read, and spent many hours talking with Edward. He led fascinating discussions on theology, philosophy, history, politics, and law.

After returning home from vacation, Elizabeth spent most of her time in leisurely activities. She rode horses, read, and visited friends and relatives. She also began to spend time with the law students in her father's office. She enjoyed a good argument with them, particularly if it dealt with the topic of women.

On several occasions Elizabeth took a trip to her cousin Gerrit Smith's house in Peterboro, New York. She had visited there as a child, but then she was not impressed by his importance as a well-known reformer and abolitionist. Now she found his ideas and activities much more interesting. She also liked to meet and talk with Gerrit's friends, several of whom were also involved in the antislavery movement. One of them was a public speaker named Henry Brewster Stanton.

Elizabeth was thrilled by the stories Henry told about his antislavery lectures. When she heard him speak in public, she remarked that he had the rare ability to make an audience both laugh and cry.

Henry was also a handsome man and Elizabeth soon fell in love with him. A month after they met, they were engaged. At first her father disapproved of their courtship, but she eventually convinced him of their love for each other. Nevertheless, most of the Cady family was not present when the couple was married on May 10, 1840. Some of them had opposed the marriage and Elizabeth had decided not to risk trouble.

The minister who performed the ceremony was shocked by a change the bride and groom requested him to make in it. They asked him to omit the word *obey* when he had them exchange their vows. Elizabeth refused to enter marriage with a promise to obey anyone. "Our marriage is a partnership of equals," she explained.

The newlyweds began their honeymoon in London, so that Henry could serve as a delegate to the World Anti-Slavery Convention. Later they traveled in England, Scotland, Ireland, and France, where Henry gave antislavery lectures and wrote articles for American newspapers. Elizabeth became very angry at the convention because women were not allowed to take part in it. But she found comfort in talking with the American women who had been sent as delegates. Like her, they also believed in equality of the sexes.

The woman delegate with whom she spent the most time was a charming and educated Quaker named Lucretia Mott. Lucretia was twenty years older than Elizabeth, but they shared many of the same views. Elizabeth talked to her about social reform, theology, and women's rights. She also went to hear Lucretia preach at a London church, the first time she had heard a woman address an audience that included men.

Elizabeth and Lucretia got along so well that they agreed to hold a woman's rights convention when they returned to the United States. This convention did not take place for several years, though, because both women became involved in other matters.

The Stantons returned to America in the fall of 1840. For the next two years Henry studied law with Judge Cady in Johnstown. During this period Elizabeth had plenty of time for horseback riding, reading, and thinking. In 1842 she gave birth to her first child, Daniel. When Henry had finished his training, the Stantons moved to Boston, where he had decided to open an office. Following the move, two more sons were born, Henry in 1844 and Gerrit in 1845.

The four years Elizabeth spent in Boston were very satisfying for her. She continued to enjoy motherhood, cooking, and gardening. She also met a good many interesting people, such as poets Ralph Waldo Emerson and John Greenleaf Whittier, as well as numerous abolitionists and statesmen. In addition, she attended lectures, concerts, theater programs, and meetings to discuss prison reform and temperance. "My mental powers were kept at the highest tension," she said of this period in her life.

About the same time as the Stantons' move to Boston, Judge Cady moved to Albany, New York, the state capital. While visiting her father there, Elizabeth became involved in the effort to pass the Married Woman's Property Bill, which had been pending in the state legislature since 1836.

Remembering the frustrating cases of the women

who had visited her father's office, Elizabeth felt strongly about changing the existing property laws. They were based on the belief that a woman was unable to understand figures or care for herself, and therefore needed protection. A wife had no say in matters relating to her own property. All that she owned, even jewelry, belonged to her husband and could be claimed by him or sold and used to pay off debts. If she worked, everything that she earned went to her husband. If she fled from home because her husband beat her, she could take nothing, not even her children.

Elizabeth talked to many legislators in Albany about the unfairness of the state's property laws. She also presented them with petitions signed by people who supported changes in these laws. Finally in April 1848 a bill was passed that allowed married women to have real estate in their own names. It did not change all the aspects of the laws that Elizabeth and other reformers had fought against, but it was a victory for the cause of women's rights.

A year before the property act passed, a major change occurred in Elizabeth's life. Boston's damp climate had proved too harsh for Henry, who suffered from chronic lung congestion, and so the Stantons were forced to move. They chose a small town in central New York called Seneca Falls. It was close to a railroad line to Albany and Johnstown, and Judge Cady owned a house there. He gave this house to the Stantons, and they lived in it for the next fifteen years. During this time four more children were born to them—Theodore in 1851, Margaret in 1852, Harriet in 1856, and Robert in 1859.

At first Elizabeth was occupied with settling into the new house and arranging for servants. However, once Henry established his new office, he began to travel a good deal and Elizabeth soon found herself alone. Bored with housework and lacking intelligent conversation, she spent many hours thinking back to the activities she had been involved in when she lived in Boston. More than ever she wanted to become active again. Yet as she later said, "I could not see what to do, or where to begin."

Then one July day in 1848 something happened that gave a new direction to her life. She received an invitation to come to a tea party at the house of Mrs. Jane Hunt. When she arrived, she was delighted to find her friend Lucretia Mott there. Lucretia's sister Martha Wright and another woman, Mary Ann McClintock, were also present.

The day proved to be an exciting one for Elizabeth. For it seemed that the five reformers all had similar ideas and grievances, or complaints, about the position of women in their society. They were especially moved by what Elizabeth had to say. In her words, "My discontent ... moved us all to prompt action; and we decided, then and there, to call a 'Woman's Rights Convention.' "

Within a few hours the women agreed to place the following notice of the meeting in the *Seneca County Courier:* "WOMAN'S RIGHTS CONVENTION—A convention to discuss the social, civil, and religious condition and rights of woman, will be held in the Wesleyan Chapel, at Seneca Falls, N.Y., on Wednesday and Thursday the 19th and 20th of July, current; commencing at 10 o'clock A.M. During the first day the meeting will be exclusively for women, who are earnestly invited to attend. The public generally are invited the second day, when Lucretia Mott, of Philadelphia, and other ladies and gentlemen, will address the convention."

Before Wednesday the five women met once more to draw up an agenda and a list of resolutions. They were full of ideas, but they had a difficult time organizing and focusing them into clear and dramatic statements. Finally Elizabeth suggested that they follow the form and phrasing of the Declaration of Independence. Her idea lead to a Declaration of Sentiments, in which she wrote, "We hold these truths to be self-evident: that all men and women are created equal."

Elizabeth also drew up a list of resolutions which criticized the laws that discriminated against women. When the convention met, everyone completely agreed with all of these resolutions, except for the ninth one. It urged the women of the United States to seek the right to vote.

Even the convention's founders were shocked at this idea. They were certain that calling for the right to vote would ruin their cause. Lucretia tried to talk Elizabeth out of making the resolution, but Elizabeth held firm. The only way to change the position of women, she concluded, was to change the laws. And the only way to get the laws changed was by having women vote for the people who made them.

Not even Henry could persuade his stubborn wife to withdraw the resolution. He had always supported her, but this time he felt she had gone too far. In fact, he was so outraged and humiliated that on the first day of the convention he rode his horse out of town!

On July 20 Elizabeth stepped before the crowd of 300 men and women who had gathered in the Methodist chapel. Although she was shaking from stagefright, she soon forgot her fear and spoke forcefully on the importance of voting power. At the end of her speech she received quite a surprise. By a small margin, her controversial ninth resolution won enough support to pass.

Among the one hundred men and women who signed the Declaration of Sentiments was young Charlotte Woodward, who worked in a local glove factory. Of all the women who were present that day, she was the only one who lived to cast a vote when Congress finally ratified a woman suffrage amendment. That was not until 1920—seventy-two years after the convention in Seneca Falls.

The first women's rights convention was termed a grand success, and a second one was called two weeks later in Rochester, New York. A good deal was accomplished at this meeting, but now the women saw how much work lay ahead of them.

Even though the conventions were successful, Elizabeth was amazed at public reaction to them. "No words could express our astonishment on finding . . . that what seemed to us so timely, so rational, and so sacred should be a subject for sarcasm and ridicule to the entire press of the nation." Newspapers called the meetings a "tomfoolery convention" that had been attended by "amazons" and "sour old maids."

In Philadelphia, the *Public Ledger and Daily Transcript* tried to undermine the idea that women needed power. According to one of its writers, "mothers, grandmothers, aunts, and sweethearts manage everything. Men have nothing to do but listen and obey." Other papers tried to make the meetings seem unimportant. The *Rochester Daily Advertiser* told its readers that the women "appear extremely dull and uninteresting, and aside from their novelty, hardly worth notice."

Despite the fact that the publicity was negative, news of the conventions caught the attention of women in other cities. One of them not only became Elizabeth's strongest ally in the movement for women's rights, but also her closest friend. Her name was Susan B. Anthony.

Elizabeth devoted two chapters of her autobiography to Susan, whom she called her "good angel" and a "sincere, concentrated worker." Explaining how they complemented each other in their work, Elizabeth said that she was best with ideas and words, and Susan with facts, statistics, and analysis. "Our speeches may be considered the united product of our two brains," Elizabeth wrote. But Elizabeth usually gave the speeches, while Susan arranged for lectures and organized committees. In Elizabeth's words, "I forged the thunderbolts and she fired them."

At the time of their meeting in 1851, Susan was living in Rochester, New York. Several years before she had given up a fifteen-year teaching career to give more time to reform causes. The young Quaker woman's main interests then were in the temperance and antislavery movements.

In 1852, after being snubbed at a men's state temperance convention, the two women set up the New York Woman's Temperance Society. At its first meeting Elizabeth was elected president and Susan secretary. During the convention, Elizabeth and many women wore short hair and the newly-designed bloomer outfits. Named after Amelia Bloomer, editor of a temperance journal called *The Lily,* this dress consisted of a short skirt and long, loose pants gathered at the ankles. It was much more comfortable than the long skirts and heavy petticoats women were usually expected to wear. Many people were outraged at seeing women in bloomers, however. Hecklers even threw eggs and stones at women who wore them.

Shocking as the women's outfits and hairstyles were, the public was less stunned by them than by Elizabeth's speech. For in it she proposed that a woman should be able to divorce her husband if his drinking was ruining her life. "Let no woman remain in the relation of wife with the confirmed drunkard," she said. "Let no drunkard be the father of her children."

Elizabeth knew that a woman had no legal protection against an alcoholic husband. He could do anything to get liquor—take the family's money, apprentice the children, sell the family's property—and she was powerless to stop him. Even if he beat his wife or their children, the law did not allow her to leave him.

Yet most women were as astonished as men at such open talk of divorce. In fact, they often scorned the ideas put forth by Elizabeth and her friends as strongly as men. Elizabeth believed these women had been used to unjust treatment for so long that they couldn't imagine a different way of life.

Despite being criticized for her stand on divorce, Elizabeth continued to speak on it. In 1854 she addressed the joint judiciary committees of the New York legislature on the issue. She was very nervous about giving this speech because it was her first chance to talk to the state's lawmakers. She became even more upset when her father asked her to stop at his home in Albany and read the speech to him before she delivered it.

Judge Cady was opposed to the women's movement and deeply hurt by the active role Elizabeth had taken in it. She was very worried that he would condemn her speech. But as she read it to him, she saw that it moved him. And when she finished, he complimented her and even offered to help with some fine points of law.

Speaking to the legislature was a gratifying experience for Elizabeth. She began by demanding that women be given full legal and social rights. Then she movingly described the cruel effects that the laws concerning marriage and property had on women. Next she argued that since men and women had similar natures, they should each have the same legal rights. Finally she suggested that if women were to help better society, their "moral power ought to speak, not only in the home but through the ballot box."

Needless to say, Elizabeth's speech created a great deal of discussion. Later she gave others on the same issue. After hearing one of them some women in Albany disapprovingly asked what she did with her children while she was on a speaking tour. In this case she could confidently reply that they were in a nearby hotel room with the family's nurse. Often, however, she did have to be away from her husband and children for weeks at a time. On occasion she felt very guilty about leaving her family in the care of others. Yet she always did her best to balance her work and her home life.

Elizabeth addressed the New York legislature again in 1860. This time she was instrumental in helping to pass a bill that allowed women to keep their own wages, to make their own contracts, and to have joint guardianship of their children. Elizabeth felt pleased that some progress was being made toward giving women full legal rights. Unfortunately, her father died shortly before her address and could not share in her triumph.

When the Civil War began, the movement for women's rights came to a standstill. Its leaders lent their support to gaining freedom for the slaves. In addition, many of them did what they could to aid soldiers and support the war effort.

In 1862 Elizabeth and her family moved to New York City where Henry had been appointed a custom's inspector. After settling in the city, she took up the cause of women's rights more actively than ever before. Both she and Susan Anthony feared that the gains women had already made would be lost or forgotten.

The war to free the slaves presented Elizabeth and Susan with a difficult problem: Should their first duty be to win rights for blacks or for women? Susan felt that all of their energies should be put into the women's movement. At first, though, Elizabeth felt that they should give most of their time to the antislavery cause. Later she admitted Susan had been right. For women were intentionally excluded from the laws that were finally passed to give blacks citizenship and voting rights. The Fourteenth Amendment to the U.S. Constitution, which made blacks citizens, stated that only adult males could vote in federal elections. The Fifteenth Amendment, which guaranteed blacks the suffrage, also applied only to men. Under it citizens could not be denied the right to vote because of their "race, color, or previous condition of servitude." Women would be prohibited from voting on the basis of their sex.

Following the war, Elizabeth decided to show up the unfairness of these laws by running for Congress. She had learned that while women did not have the right to vote, they did have the right to hold office. She presented herself as a candidate for the House of Representatives from the Eighth District of New York City. "My creed is free speech, free press, free men, and free trade—the cardinal points of democracy," she declared. Despite receiving only twenty-four votes, she thought her candidacy was a good way to draw attention to the women's movement.

By the late 1860s Elizabeth was leaving her husband and children at home with a housekeeper more and more. But she would not give up the battle for suffrage. She and Susan continued to travel under all kinds of conditions and through all kinds of weather.

Some progress toward their goal was made when a women's suffrage amendment to the Kansas constitution was put up for a vote in 1867. Elizabeth and Susan went there to campaign for this amendment, following efforts by Lucy Stone and other women. They spoke wherever people would gather and listen—in schools, churches, and the open air.

Elizabeth had once had romantic ideas about pioneer life. But she quickly learned that there was nothing romantic about it. She made her way from town to town in a mule-drawn carriage, many times losing her way because there were no roads or guideposts. Often she slept in insect-infested beds and went for days without finding suitable food to eat.

One night she decided to sleep in the carriage, preferring it to the bed she saw in a settler's house. She had just fallen into a gentle slumber when the carriage suddenly began to roll and shake, and a "chorus of pronounced grunts" filled the air. The carriage had been surrounded by long-nosed black pigs, who were using its iron steps as scratching posts. At first she tried to drive the pigs off with a whip, worrying that their fleas would get into the wagon. But the pigs were so persistent that she finally gave up and went to sleep. "I had a sad night of it," she later wrote, "and never tried the carriage again."

As miserable as the traveling conditions were, she would not turn back. The battle to get the vote for women in Kansas was too important to give up on. The main difficulty Elizabeth and Susan faced was lack of support from Republican political leaders and influential newspapers. The Republicans, who had come to power just before the Civil War, thought it was in their party's interest to gain the vote for blacks. They did not want to offend Kansas voters by asking that the suffrage be given to both blacks and women. Important newspapers also felt that blacks should be given the right to vote before women received it.

Abandoned by the Republicans and the newspapers, Elizabeth and Susan worked hard to convince voters to support the suffrage for both women and blacks. But they could not overcome strong opposition from liquor manufacturers, who feared that women would vote for temperance laws, and German settlers, who thought a woman's place was in the home. On election day, voters overwhelmingly said no to giving the suffrage to either women or blacks.

During their campaign, Elizabeth and Susan met a man who was eager to help them. He was George Francis Train, a railroad developer, a Democrat, and an opponent of black rights. Many of the women on the lecture circuit were opposed to his presence, but Elizabeth and Susan found him pleasant and entertaining. Besides, he offered to finance a weekly newspaper in which the women could express their views. Such a publication had long been Susan's dream, and she gladly accepted his offer. She and Elizabeth named their new journal *The Revolution.* Susan was its business manager, and Elizabeth and Parker Pillsbury its editors.

The Revolution had a short two-and-a-half-year life, but during that time it caused quite a stir. It attacked the Fourteenth and Fifteenth Amendments, detailed cases of discrimination against women, and openly discussed rape, prostitution, and wife beating. Many suffragists thought the paper was too extreme, however, and disagreement over it and other issues split the women's movement.

As a result, Elizabeth and Susan formed their own organization, the National Woman Suffrage Association, in 1869, with Elizabeth as acting president. The association's goal was to obtain a national woman suffrage amendment to the U.S. Constitution. The other suffragists, including Lucy Stone, formed the more moderate American Woman Suffrage Association, and printed their own newspaper. Their goal was to work for suffrage city by city and state by state.

These two organizations remained separate for twenty years. During this time, the women's movement suffered from a lack of unity. Yet each group felt that it was taking the right course.

Despite the problems resulting from the split in the women's movement and the failure of *The Revolution,* Elizabeth and Susan carried on their work. They immediately began efforts for the passage of a sixteenth amendment to the U.S. Constitution that would give all citizens the right to vote, regardless of sex. This attempt failed, however. Nevertheless, neither of them gave up hope that women would gain the suffrage, and they continued to campaign on its behalf.

One night while the two friends were crossing the Mississippi River in Iowa, the boat they were on became icebound. The passengers were crowded, hungry, and upset. At last some men who had earlier been talking with Elizabeth and Susan called out, "Speech on woman suffrage!"

The two women quickly obliged them. At midnight, in the middle of the river, they spoke on the suffrage and led a lively debate on the issue. By the time the boat landed a few passengers had accepted their views. And everyone on board was glad for the way in which the discussion had helped to pass the time.

Besides giving speeches on the suffrage, Elizabeth and Susan also tried a more direct approach. Susan registered and voted in the 1872 national election. Eight years later Elizabeth forced officials in Tenafly, New Jersey, where she had moved in 1868, to let her vote. Nothing happened to Elizabeth as a result of this action. Susan, however, was arrested and brought to trial. Judged guilty, she was fined one hundred dollars, but she refused to pay the money and the charges against her were dropped.

During the next two decades, Elizabeth began to devote more time to writing. Along with Susan and another woman, Matilda Joslyn Gage, she spent five years writing and editing three thick volumes of the *History of Woman Suffrage*. She also wrote articles for various magazines.

When her work on the history was done, Elizabeth spent a good deal of time traveling to visit her children and grandchildren in the United States and Europe. Her husband Henry's failing health prevented his accompanying her, but by then they were both used to long separations. By the time of his death in 1887, Elizabeth had become involved in an international women's reform movement and was a well-known figure outside the United States.

During her eightieth year she started work on her autobiography. Also that year Susan and the National Council of Women, an organization composed of twenty American reform groups, arranged a large celebration for Elizabeth on her birthday. Thousands of people came to a rented opera house in New York City to honor her. There she sat "queen among women" beneath an arch of white flowers decorated with pink flowers that spelled out her name.

At the time of this celebration, Elizabeth took a long look back on her life. She reviewed "its march and battles on the highways of experience and counted its defeats and victories." Over the decades, she saw, social customs had changed, laws had been modified, and the vote had been given to women in three states: Wyoming, Utah, and Colorado. There was still a long way to go, but an important beginning had been made.

In the fall of 1902, now blind and in the care of her family in New York City, Elizabeth Cady Stanton died. Not many years before her death she had stated, "My life has been one long struggle to do and say what I know to be right and true. I would not take back one brave word indeed. My only regret is that I have not been braver and bolder and truer in the honest conviction of my soul."

I MUST SPEAK FOR THE WOMEN

LUCY STONE: A leader in the women's movement for nearly fifty years, she helped organize the First National Woman's Rights Convention and the American Woman Suffrage Association.

Late in August of 1843 a packet boat made its way west across Lake Erie. Lucy Stone stood on its deck, along with freight, horses, and a few other passengers. She was preparing to sleep out there because she could not afford a stateroom for the night. The long trip from Massachusetts to Ohio by stagecoach, boat, and railcar had already cost more than sixteen dollars, and every cent counted.

Spending the night outside was only a small inconvenience to twenty-five-year-old Lucy, though. Or so it seemed when she thought about the wonderful adventure that lay ahead of her—a college education! For she was on her way to Oberlin, then the only college in the nation that admitted women on an equal basis with men.

Lucy had worked for nine years to save enough money for her college expenses. Her father, who was opposed to educating women, had refused to contribute a penny toward her school fees or transportation. In fact, she had been forced to borrow money from him just to complete enough schooling to earn a living as a teacher.

But those nine years of struggle were behind her now, and as the night came on, she thought only of the future. Soon she put her trunk and carpetbag down on the deck, lay down, and slept soundly through the night as the boat continued on its way.

Late the next day she arrived at the few rundown gray buildings that made up the Oberlin campus. Gloomy as they appeared, she was anxious to begin classes in them. For then she would reach her goal of becoming an educated and independent woman.

Beyond that, Lucy had no other plans. Yet in a short time she became one of America's most important and effective leaders in the movement for women's rights. Her work in this cause has rightly been called "a striking example of a single-hearted and lifelong devotion to a great idea."

Lucy's childhood experiences had much to do with her devotion to the women's movement. She was born on a farm near West Brookfield, Massachusetts, on August 13, 1818. Her mother, Hannah Matthews Stone, was a quiet woman who uncomplainingly cooked, cleaned, sewed, churned butter, and almost single-handedly brought up seven children. Her father, Francis Stone, a tanner as well as a farmer, was a vigorous man who ruled both his wife and children. "There was only one will in our home, and that was my father's," Lucy recalled.

When Lucy was born, her mother said, "Oh dear! I am sorry it is a girl. A woman's life is so hard!" And indeed it was, as Lucy soon learned. For even as a child she had to drive the cows out to pasture, carry water and wood, help her mother weave cloth, and, with her sisters, sew shoes that were sold for four cents a pair.

In spite of all this hard work, Lucy was given some time for pleasure. Along with the other children — Francis, William Bowman, Eliza, Rhoda, Luther, and Sarah — she jumped rope or played with the family's dog. After her school lessons, she ran barefoot through the fields, studying wildflowers, trees, and birds.

One summer Lucy was walking through a field when she came upon a large snake. Many children would have run away at the sight of this creature. But Lucy grabbed a big rock, drew near to the snake, and killed it. She was never afraid for herself, a trait that helped to make her a courageous reformer.

Reading was another activity that young Lucy enjoyed. One time her love of reading got her in trouble, though. A stagecoach often passed by her schoolhouse. When it did, the passengers would sometimes throw out tracts and pamphlets for the students to read. On one occasion, Lucy was so eager to get the reading material that she climbed out an open window in order to reach it before anyone else. She won the race, but she angered her teacher, who said, "You must come in as you went out." An embarrassed Lucy had to climb back into the building through the same window she had just gone out of.

Lucy couldn't find much to read at home. Aside from the Bible, the family owned few books, and they were generally reserved for the boys, a fact Lucy strongly resented. She couldn't understand why she should be treated differently than her brothers. Luther, for example, was neither as quick nor as fearless as she was, yet he was always shown more favor.

Lucy's anger at being unfairly treated eventually turned to despair. For while she could see that "the laws and the customs were against . . . women, . . . it had never occurred to her that God could be against them." Yet she discovered that even the Bible said that women must submit to their husbands. "Thy desire shall be to thy husband, and he shall rule over thee," it stated.

After reading these words Lucy ran to her mother and asked what she could take to kill herself. Her shocked mother tried to explain that because the first woman, Eve, had disobeyed God, all women had been cursed. That is, God set men over women as a punishment for Eve's sin. This explanation calmed Lucy down, but she still found it difficult to be as meek and submissive as her mother was.

The more Lucy thought about what she had read, the more she became determined to study Greek and Hebrew to find out if the Bible had been translated correctly. This determination meant, of course, that she would have to go to college.

"Is the child crazy?" her father asked when she announced her plans. Lucy paid little attention to that comment and similar ones that followed. Instead, she began reading her brothers' school books. When she wanted a special book for herself, she went out into the fields, picked berries and chestnuts, and sold them to pay for it. Buying her own book gave her great satisfaction. "I felt a prouder sense of triumph than I have ever known since," she said. Thereafter she always earned her own book money. No one could deny her an education that way!

At the age of sixteen Lucy began teaching school, living with her students' families as was the common practice then. She earned one dollar a week at the start. Eventually her salary was raised to sixteen dollars a month, but it was still far below the amount paid the men teachers. And it was too little for her to save much for a college education. But she would not give up that goal.

As time passed, Lucy became more and more angry at the way her society denied women an education. One day she was at a meeting of her church's sewing circle, stitching a shirt to raise money for a needy theology student. A well-known educator, Mary Lyon, had been invited to speak to the group, and she talked about the importance of educating women. Lucy listened carefully, thinking about the points made in the speech. Then she asked herself why she was helping to raise money for a man. Wasn't her own education just as important? Indeed it was, she decided, and tossing down the shirt, she left the meeting.

Another incident convinced her that women should have the right to speak out on important issues. The members of her Congregational church were voting on expelling a deacon who had spoken out against slavery. Lucy, already in sympathy with the abolitionist movement, raised her hand against ousting the man. But her hand was not counted because, as her minister scornfully explained, women were not voting members. She was advised to put her hand down so that the vote could be taken properly.

Five more votes were taken at the meeting, and Lucy raised her hand each time. She could not force the men to count her opinion, but she wanted to protest their treatment of women. Years later she vividly recalled how "one uncounted hand" had made her point.

In 1837 an organization of Congregational ministers meeting in North Brookfield, Massachusetts, where Lucy was then teaching, issued a "Pastoral Letter." It was sent out to warn people in the Congregational churches of Massachusetts about Sarah and Angelina Grimké. They were sisters from South Carolina who were publicly speaking out against slavery.

Lucy listened in disbelief as the letter condemning the two women was read to a crowd that had gathered in the North Brookfield church. They certainly did not sound dangerous to her, as the letter claimed. In fact, they sounded like the kind of women she would like to meet. For by daring to speak before audiences that included both men and women, they, too, had challenged the idea that women must keep their place.

Hearing the ministers' letter made Lucy's anger "blaze." She told her cousin that "if I ever had anything to say in public, I should say it, and all the more because of that Pastoral Letter."

This letter also reinforced Lucy's determination to get a college education. Strangely enough, she did not apply on her own. It was such an unacceptable practice for a woman to attend college that she wanted to make certain that nothing went wrong. And so she asked her brother Bowman, now a Congregational minister, to apply on her behalf. He did so, and Lucy was accepted immediately.

Because Lucy entered Oberlin at the age of twenty-five, she was somewhat older than many students. As a result, her interests were widespread, ranging from academic subjects to reform movements. She was especially concerned about the movement to free the slaves. She had become an avid reader of the abolitionist newspaper *The Liberator*, and a follower of the beliefs of its publisher, William Lloyd Garrison.

Being one of Garrison's followers created some problems for Lucy. Her first roomate, for example, was a young girl from South Carolina. The girl's father, a slaveholder, was afraid that his daughter might become an abolitionist. He forbade her to discuss the subject of slavery with Lucy or anyone else.

Lucy managed to get along with her roommate, though, and she soon settled down to college life. The school only charged one dollar a week for board, but that was still too costly for her. To cut expenses, she began doing her own cooking in her room, which saved fifty cents a week. In addition, she did housework in the Ladies Hall for three cents an hour. She didn't want her lessons to suffer because she had to work, and so she propped her books against a ledge and studied Greek while she washed dishes.

Because of her previous teaching experience, Lucy was allowed to teach in the college's preparatory school for two-and-a-half hours each day. Here she was paid twelve and a half cents an hour to hold classes for adult black men, many of them former slaves. Because Ohio was a border state between the free and slave territories, a number of runaway slaves had settled there.

Lucy was more than eager to help the black men. The class, however, was not so enthusiastic. On the first day one man rose and declared that it was wrong for grown men to be taught by a young woman. Reading and writing are so important, Lucy replied, that it shouldn't matter who the teacher is. Finally she persuaded them to give her a chance, and in a short time they came to respect and admire her.

Lucy had a very busy schedule during her first two years at Oberlin. Her last two years were made somewhat easier by a loan from her father, who had come to respect her courage. Remembering his own hard times, he wrote, "There will be no trouble about the money; you can have what you will need, without studying nights, or working for eight cents an hour."

Although Lucy was generally pleased with the education she was receiving, she sometimes clashed with Oberlin's authorities. The first time came when she removed her bonnet during the long church service that all students were required to attend each Sunday. Wearing the bonnet gave her a very bad headache, and she took it off to feel better. The school's authorities were shocked by her action. They believed that the Bible taught that women must keep their heads covered in church.

The Oberlin Ladies' Board, a group of professor's wives, decided that Lucy must be dealt with. They summoned her to meet with them, and told her she was disobeying the Bible by removing her bonnet. But Lucy replied that if she kept it on, "I am good for nothing all the rest of the day. What account shall I give to God of my wasted Sunday afternoons?" This clever reply was hard to answer. Finally the board agreed that Lucy could take off her bonnet if her headache became unbearably painful. But it directed her to sit in the last row of the chapel during religious services.

Lucy also became disappointed and disturbed when some of Oberlin's professors attacked William Lloyd

Garrison's call for the immediate emancipation of all slaves. Lucy was one of Garrison's followers, and she shared his deep feelings about slavery. She had even made up her mind to become a public speaker like him and his abolitionist friends.

This decision led to another problem. Even though Oberlin admitted both men and women, only men were allowed to give speeches in public. As a result, Lucy could not take part in her speech class's weekly debates. It is enough for women to learn from men, she was told. But how could she become a public lecturer without gaining experience in speaking and debating?

Luckily she found a friend and ally in a new student named Antoinette Brown. Antoinette also wanted to develop her speaking skills because she planned to become a Congregational minister. (After facing a great many obstacles, she was finally ordained as the first woman minister in the United States.)

When Antoinette was traveling to Oberlin, she was warned against associating with Lucy Stone, "a young woman of strange and dangerous opinions." That warning only made her want to seek Lucy out, and they became steadfast friends. Later they also became sisters-in-law.

Lucy and Antoinette jointly complained about the speech class policy. Finally they were allowed to debate, but only against each other. Their debate attracted a huge crowd because most people on the campus had never heard a woman give a speech. But it outraged the Ladies' Board, which immediately banned public debates by women.

The ban didn't stop the two friends, though, because they organized a secret women's debating society. At first its members practiced in the woods, taking turns to watch for intruders. In the winter they persuaded a black woman, the mother of one of Lucy's pupils, to let them meet in her house.

Lucy gave her first public speech to a group of blacks at Oberlin. Each year this group celebrated the freeing of the slaves in the British West Indies, an event which had occurred in 1833. Lucy spoke to the group on the subject of rejoicing for freedom.

When the Ladies' Board found out about the speech, Lucy was asked if her appearance on a platform with men had not "embarrassed and frightened" her. "I was not afraid of them a bit," she replied.

Despite being criticized by the board, Lucy continued to believe that women should be allowed to speak in public. As a leading member of her graduating class of 1847, she was entitled to write an essay for the commencement ceremony. But the school refused to let her read. She could write the essay, the authorities said, but it would have to be read by a male professor. Lucy turned this idea down. Many of her classmates joined in her protest, and in the end none of the protesters wrote or read papers.

William Lloyd Garrison recognized Lucy's spark and spirit when he met her during a visit to Oberlin. "She is a very superior young woman," he wrote in a letter to his wife, "and has a soul as free as the air, and is preparing to go forth as a lecturer." Other visiting abolitionist speakers like Stephen and Abby Kelly Foster shared Garrison's feelings about Lucy. Later Abby helped Lucy get her first job as lecturer for the Massachusetts Anti-Slavery Society.

Everyone in Lucy's family, except two brothers,

tried to discourage a speaking career. They wanted her to teach instead of becoming a public lecturer. But Lucy was not about to change her mind.

Writing to her mother, she said, "If in this hour of the world's need I should refuse to lend my aid, . . . I should have no right to think myself a Christian, and I should forever despise Lucy Stone. If, while I hear the wild shriek of the slave mother robbed of her little ones, . . .I do not open my mouth for the dumb, am I not guilty?"

Lucy also told her mother that "there are no trials so great as they suffer who neglect or refuse to do what they believe is their duty. I expect to plead not for the slave only, but for suffering humanity everywhere. ESPECIALLY DO I MEAN TO LABOR FOR THE ELEVATION OF MY SEX."

Lucy began her long and difficult lecturing career as a paid speaker for the Massachusetts Anti-Slavery Society in 1849. Abby Kelley Foster and the society's general agent, Samuel May, helped her get started. She was an effective speaker from the moment she mounted a platform, and her soft and musical sounding voice soon became famous.

Lucy's work for the society was difficult. She had to learn to overcome the rigors of traveling in open wagons, especially during cold and rainy weather. She also had to learn to advertise her work by tacking up advance notices of her speeches, despite the fact that they were often ripped down.

In addition, Lucy had to endure a great many humiliations. Once a man hurled a prayer book at the lecture platform and struck her in the head. Another time someone threw pepper into the meeting hall, causing the speakers and the audience to suffer a sneezing spell. And on still another occasion, one bitter winter day someone stuck a hose through the window and turned icy water on Lucy. Cold and shivering, she went right on with her speech!

It was not always easy to say whether the people who performed such acts were opposed to Lucy's anti-slavery message, to women speakers, or to both. Lucy didn't worry about the matter, though, and carried on her work. She did find it difficult to remain silent about women's rights, however, and soon began to speak about freedom for women as well as blacks.

Samuel May, the agent who had hired her for the Anti-Slavery Society, was not pleased with this development. He sympathized with Lucy's views about discrimination against women, but he reminded her that she was being paid six dollars a week to speak on abolition.

"I was a woman before I was an abolitionist," Lucy replied. "I must speak for the women."

Because she had become one of the society's best speakers, a compromise was made. Lucy could speak for women during the week, but she must devote weekends to preaching against slavery.

In nineteenth-century America, public lectures not only served to educate people but to entertain them. Since books and newspapers were not always available, and there was no radio or television, many people were glad to have guest lecturers come to their towns. Some people traveled many miles to attend a lecture series and stayed on to listen to as many speakers as possible.

When Lucy spoke, women often remained afterwards to talk to her. Many of them poured out stories of the wrongs they had suffered. Sometimes these stories gave Lucy fresh material for her next speeches.

One evening Lucy appeared with the Hutchinson family, a group of antislavery singers who charged admission to their performances. They shared the evening's proceeds with her, and she was delighted to have the extra money. It even turned out to be enough to buy herself a new cloak, which she badly needed. Thereafter, instead of taking up a collection at her lectures, she always charged a fee of twelve and a half cents. This fee not only provided her with an income, but it also helped to keep out hecklers and hoodlums. In three years she earned seven thousand dollars, a huge sum for those times.

By that time the first women's rights convention had met in Seneca Falls, New York, and had given rise to similar meetings in other cities. In 1850 Lucy attended the first National Woman's Rights Convention in Worcester, Massachusetts. There she met her former school friend Antoinette Brown, as well as other important women, including Lucretia Mott and the ex-slave Sojourner Truth.

Lucy almost missed this convention because she was stricken with typhoid fever, an illness from which she nearly died. She recovered in time, however, and set out to attend the meeting in Massachusetts. On the way she stopped in Cincinnati, Ohio, and while there she met a hardware merchant and abolitionist named Henry Blackwell. He was immediately "struck by her brightness and charm of manner," but Lucy left Cincinnati completely unaware of his feelings toward her. She certainly couldn't have imagined then that he would someday enter her life forever.

During the next few years Lucy attended both anti-slavery and women's rights conventions. In 1853 she was a featured speaker at antislavery meetings in New York and Boston. Henry Blackwell went to both of these meetings, and also met Lucy at the antislavery society's offices in Boston. Impressed by Lucy's "beauty, charm, and eloquence," he made up his mind to marry her.

Henry approached William Lloyd Garrison and asked him for a formal letter of introduction to give to Lucy. Garrison warned Henry that Lucy had already turned down other offers of marriage. Nevertheless, he wrote the letter.

Lucy had long ago decided that she would never marry. Yet she found it difficult to resist Henry, seven years younger than herself, and an energetic, witty, and worldly man. Furthermore, he understood women who wanted to make something of themselves. His sister Elizabeth was already famous as the first woman doctor in the country.

As Henry continued to romance Lucy, she came to care a good deal for him. Nevertheless, she refused to marry him. "Marriage is to a woman a state of slavery," she said. Henry, however, would not give up. When they were apart he wrote her long love letters. He also tried over and over to convince her that they could combine marriage and work. Still, Lucy held firm. She wished to remain single and independent.

One day Henry surprised Lucy with a visit to her home. He found her standing on a kitchen table, white-washing the ceiling. She was wearing a bloomer outfit, a comfortable but widely ridiculed trouser-dress combination. After Lucy introduced him to her family, Henry helped her prepare dinner by peeling potatoes, while she cut up carrots. All in all, it turned out to be a pleasant day. But "submit" to marriage? That was still out of the question.

Then at last something happened that prompted Lucy to change her mind. She learned that Henry had been involved in the daring rescue of a young slave girl. The incident took place in Salem, Ohio, where an anti-slavery convention was being held. While Henry was speaking, word came that a westbound train passing through Salem would be carrying a slave girl. She was the property of a man and a woman who were returning with her to Tennessee. The girl was not legally bound to go back with them, however. According to a recent ruling by the Ohio supreme court, slaves brought into the state by their masters could gain freedom merely by expressing a desire for it.

Henry was in the crowd that met the train at the station. When it stopped, he and several other abolitionists stormed inside the train and asked the child if she wished to remain free. She answered yes, and in a flash Henry lifted the little girl from her seat. He was then grabbed by another passenger, but he managed to hold the man off while his friends took the girl to safety.

This heroic action impressed Lucy more than anything Henry had yet done to win her love. In the weeks that followed, her feelings for him became stronger and stronger, although she was still uncertain about marriage. Finally, however, finding love more powerful than the fear of losing her independence, she agreed to marry Henry.

Their wedding took place on May 1, 1855, at the Stone family farm in Massachusetts. Lucy had wanted her friend Antoinette Brown, now an ordained Congregational minister, to perform the ceremony, but Antoinette was only licensed to officiate in New York State. And so Lucy's old friend, the Reverend Thomas Wentworth Higginson, married the couple before breakfast in the parlor of the farmhouse. Lucy wore a silk "ashes-of-roses color" gown and Henry a "proper white waistcoat."

Before the ceremony, Henry read a protest about marriage that he and Lucy had written. It declared that while they would love and honor each other, they disagreed with the current marriage laws. These laws gave a husband complete control over his wife's property, earnings, and activities, as well as their children. Somewhat later, Lucy also refused to change her name from Stone to Blackwell, as was the custom. "A wife should no more take her husband's name, than he should hers," she announced. Thereafter, any woman who married but kept her own name became known as a "Lucy Stoner."

The first years of their marriage were difficult for Lucy and Henry. Lucy's old fears about losing her freedom and identity returned so strongly that she began to suffer headaches again. In addition, she and Henry were often separated from each other because of Henry's business trips and reform work, and Lucy's lecturing. Furthermore, they were having financial troubles.

One summer Henry was able to convince Lucy to travel with him to Wisconsin, where he owned property. This trip turned out to be a memorable adventure for both of them. It combined the thrill of seeing beautiful scenery with the experience of living a hard frontier life. Lucy was especially struck by the hardships that pioneer women had to endure. "The women work out as much or more than the men," she wrote, "and are never allowed more than four days after the birth of a child, before they have to milk." These women were much on her mind when she gave several lectures on slavery and women's rights to Wisconsin audiences.

Some time after she and Henry returned, Lucy learned she was going to have a baby. This knowledge added to her already mixed feelings about marriage and motherhood. She remembered the years of hardship her mother had suffered, having to bear nine children and to bring up seven of them. Besides, having a baby was not always an easy or pleasant experience. Many women died in childbirth or from complications afterwards. But everything went well for Lucy and Henry, and on September 14, 1857, in their new home in Orange, New Jersey, a daughter was born to them. She was named Alice Stone Blackwell.

For the next ten years Lucy was not actively involved in the women's rights movement. She wanted to stay at home and be a good mother for Alice. When Alice was not quite three, Lucy bore another child, a boy, who, sadly, died almost immediately after birth. Lucy suffered long periods of depression following his death.

Henry's land and real estate work continued to require him to travel frequently. But neither he nor Lucy liked being separated, and in 1858 she and Alice moved to Evanston, Illinois, to be with him. Then in the summer of 1859 the family returned to Orange, New Jersey, where Lucy occasionally helped out in his real estate office.

She was frustrated at not being fully involved in working for women's rights. Yet she did manage to contribute a little to the cause. On one occasion she refused to pay a tax bill to protest women's lack of voting rights. Since she wasn't allowed to vote, she reasoned that she was being denied a right granted to male tax-payers. The state of New Jersey did not accept her argu-ment, though, and auctioned off some of her household property to get its money. Nevertheless, by standing on a principle—no taxation without representation—she gained a good deal of publicity for the women's movement.

Lucy also managed to attend a national women's rights convention in 1860. After the Civil War broke out, she helped to organize the Woman's Loyal National League. This league was instrumental in gaining passage of the Thirteenth Amendment to the U.S. Constitution, which finally put an end to slavery.

Not long afterwards, the Fourteenth Amendment was drafted. It was intended to give blacks the suffrage, or right to vote, but it was worded in such a way as to apply only to men. People who had campaigned on behalf of giving women the suffrage were angry about the proposed amendment. They wanted its backers, the abolitionists, to support a law that would give the vote to blacks and women at the same time. Many advocates of women's suffrage, including Lucy and Henry, made a trip to Washington to ask Congress to omit the word "male" from the draft.

The amendment was passed exactly the way it was written, however. Once again, women had been ignored! Now the suffrage campaign went full steam ahead, and Lucy was ready to give it all her time and energy.

In 1867 she became president of the New Jersey Woman Suffrage Association. That same year she and Henry journeyed to Kansas along with several other leaders of the women's rights movement. There they urged people to support changes in the state's constitution that would give women the suffrage. Later they did the same thing when a women's suffrage measure was placed on the Colorado ballot. Unfortunately, both proposals were defeated.

These defeats were especially discouraging to Lucy because she believed the suffrage could be won on a city-by-city, state-by-state basis. She was opposed to the view that women would get the vote more quickly if they worked for a national suffrage law. This view had led Elizabeth Cady Stanton and Susan B. Anthony to form the National Woman Suffrage Association. Lucy believed that this organization was asking for too much change at once. As a result, she and a number of other women formed a separate women's suffrage group.

Lucy's organization became known as the American Woman Suffrage Association. Soon after it was formed, she helped to secure the funds to establish its official publication, the *Woman's Journal.* Later she and Henry became the paper's editors. The journal advocated a slow, step-by-step approach to winning the suffrage. In addition, it supported many other women's causes: access to higher education, dress reform, women's clubs, and entrance into new professions and occupations.

The *Woman's Journal* went through some difficult times, but Lucy kept it going by selling advertising and by soliciting contributions. As a result of her efforts, it was published for nearly fifty years. Lucy's daughter Alice, who never married and lived until 1950, became the paper's editor-in-chief after her parents' death.

In 1883 Lucy, Henry, and Antoinette Brown

Blackwell were lecturing in the Midwest when the two women received a surprise invitation. They were asked to be guest speakers at none other than Oberlin, their old college. Once they had not been permitted to appear on a lecture platform there. Now they were going to be special guests, treated with honor and high esteem, at the school's Fourth of July celebration.

What an exciting and triumphant day it was! Lucy's speech praised the college and spoke of the gains women had made during the school's fifty-year existence. More important, she urged everyone there to support women's suffrage as strongly as they had supported women's education.

During the next ten years, Lucy's health and energy declined. A stomach disorder kept her from attending the famous Chicago World's Fair of 1893. Earlier that year, however, she had managed to make a trip to the city to help prepare the Woman's Department at the fair. While she was there, she was embarrassed to learn that a bust of her had been made for display. She even viewed it as a foolish expense. She would have preferred that the money spent on the bust had been donated to the cause of women's rights, she told friends. Later the bust was presented to the Boston Public Library.

Lucy Stone died of stomach cancer on October 18, 1893. A few weeks later, Colorado finally voted to grant women the suffrage, the second state to do so. Wyoming, which entered the Union in 1890, was the first state to give women the right to vote.

It was unfortunate for Lucy and the other dedicated pioneers of women's suffrage that they saw few results of their work. They all seemed to know, however, that important and sweeping changes were not far off, and they always viewed the future with high hopes. These hopes were finally fulfilled in 1920, when the Nineteenth Amendment, which gave women full voting rights, was added to the U.S. Constitution.

Lucy, of course, would have taken great joy in this amendment. It was the fruit of her life's work. Yet she had accomplished a great many other things. She was the first woman from Massachusetts to earn a college degree, the first woman to give an entire speech on women's rights, and the first married woman to keep her own name. For ten years she was the "morning star of the woman's rights movement," giving lectures and organizing conventions. And for the last twenty-seven years of her life she worked tirelessly for women's suffrage.

During her final illness, Lucy clipped a poem she liked from a newspaper. It expressed her wish to be "remembered [only] by what I have done." But neither Lucy Stone nor her work has been forgotten. She is remembered for her independence, determination, and courage, as well as her pioneering efforts in women's long struggle for equal rights.

Other Outstanding Women

In addition to the six women featured in this book, there are many hundreds more who have contributed greatly to the struggle for women's rights. Although it is impossible to discuss them all, here are a few more of the foremost figures in the women's movement.

SUSAN B. ANTHONY (1820-1906). This Massachusetts-born Quaker devoted nearly half her life to winning the suffrage for women. Although she frequently lectured on women's rights, her more natural talents lay in writing, editing, and organizing material. In 1877 she helped to draft a proposal that later became the basis for the Nineteenth Amendment to the U.S. Constitution, which gave women full voting rights. Susan also took direct action to win the suffrage for women by illegally voting in the 1872 national election. Her arrest, trial, and refusal to pay a fine for what she had done drew widespread attention to the suffrage issue. Toward the end of her life Susan spent eight years as president of the National American Woman Suffrage Association. She remained active until a week before her death at the age of eighty-six.

ANTOINETTE BROWN BLACKWELL (1825-1921). Antoinette was the first ordained woman minister in the United States. As a child she was very religious, and the people in her home town of Henrietta, New York, said

that she would make a wonderful minister's wife someday. But Antoinette wanted to be the preacher. To prepare herself for this work she went to Oberlin College in
Ohio. Here she made friends with her future sister-in-
law, Lucy Stone, a strong advocate of women's rights.
Antoinette hoped to earn a divinity degree at Oberlin's
theological school. She was only allowed to study at the
school, however, because the faculty did not believe
women should be ministers. Antoinette finished her stud-
ies in 1850, but she was not granted a degree. Three years
later she was ordained a Congregational minister in New
York State, but she resigned her position in 1854, finding
the church's doctrines too strict. Then she joined a Uni-
tarian church, where she sometimes preached. In 1856
she married Samuel Blackwell and settled into family
life, bringing up six children. At the age of eighty-three
she was finally awarded the degree that she had earned at
Oberlin.

HARRIOT STANTON BLATCH (1856-1940). Like
her mother Elizabeth Cady Stanton, Harriot was a
leader in the American women's suffrage movement.
While married to an Englishman and living in England,
she was influenced by the British women's rights movement. After her husband died, she returned to the United
States and sponsored tours by the leaders of the British
cause. One of them, Emmeline Pankhurst, had used
hunger strikes as a method of gaining the vote for
women in England. Harriot also became involved in
organizing women's political unions in New York State,
campaigning on the streets and in front of factory gates.
Believing that a woman needed to handle her own business affairs, she once stated that "he who steals my purse

may steal trash, but he who holds the purse strings controls my life."

AMELIA BLOOMER (1818-1894). A temperance reformer and advocate of women's rights, Amelia became famous for an outfit she began to wear in 1851. A trouser-skirt combination, she found it much more comfortable and sensible than the heavy ruffled dresses then worn by women. But the short skirt and baggy, Turkish-looking pants appeared ridiculous to the public. Nevertheless, Amelia wore her bloomers, as they came to be called, whenever she delivered speeches. She also wrote about dress reform, the suffrage, property rights, and other women's issues in *The Lily*, a temperance journal she had begun in 1849. In addition to her public work, Amelia served as deputy postmaster in Seneca Falls, New York, from 1849 to 1854. Later she and her editor-husband, Dexter Bloomer, moved to Council Bluffs, Iowa, where she continued her work in the women's movement.

MARIA WESTON CHAPMAN (1806-1885). Maria was William Lloyd Garrison's right-hand woman, helping him with his speaking engagements and with his abolitionist newspaper, *The Liberator*. Once she and Garrison were attacked by a mob at a women's antislavery society meeting in Boston that Maria had organized. The mayor of the city urged them to escape out the back of the meeting hall, but Maria said, "If this is the last bulwark of freedom, we may as well die here as anywhere." Luckily, though, she, Garrison, and all the members of the society got out of the building before they were injured or killed. Maria also gave more than twenty years of her life to the difficult task of raising funds to win freedom for blacks.

LYDIA MARIA CHILD (1802-1880). Lydia was a popular author and abolitionist. While still in her early twenties, she wrote two novels and established a magazine for children. Then in 1833 she wrote *An Appeal in Favor of That Class of Americans Called Africans*, which condemned slavery. It became a big seller almost at once, but it also offended many people. The library in Boston, where she and her lawyer husband lived, was so upset by the book that it withdrew her borrowing privileges. Furthermore, bookstores in the South stopped selling her books, and her magazine business dropped considerably. But Lydia continued to write books and pamphlets, as well as edit a national antislavery newspaper. Lydia tried to find beauty everywhere. She once said, "I have prisms in my windows to fill the room with rainbows."

PAULINA WRIGHT DAVIS (1813-1876). "We ask to be regarded, respected, and treated as human beings, of full age and natural abilities, as equal fellow sinners, and not as infants or beautiful angels." These words were written by Paulina in *The Una*, a women's rights magazine she began publishing in 1853. Shortly before that time the wealthy young widow had established herself as a leader in the women's movement. She had presided over the First National Woman's Rights Convention held in Worcester, Massachusetts. That convention was attended by Lucretia Mott, Sojourner Truth, Lucy Stone, Angelina Grimké, Ernestine Rose, Antoinette Brown, and many other well-known women. During the

1840s, Paulina campaigned for the passage of laws that would give women the right to own property. This campaign achieved some success when the New York legislature passed the Married Woman's Property Act in 1848. It gave wives control of the property they had owned before their marriage. Paulina also felt that the women of her day knew very little about their own bodies, especially in regards to birth control. Therefore, from 1845 to 1849 she gave lectures on female anatomy to many women's groups. She used a plaster figure of a female nude in these talks, and when it was uncovered, some women considered it so "indelicate" that they "ran out of the room or even fainted."

ABIGAIL KELLEY FOSTER (1810-1887). A Quaker reformer who spoke out against slavery and for women's rights, Abby was one of the most persecuted crusaders of her day. She began her career at a time when few people thought women should speak in public. As a result, New Englanders were shocked when she joined Sarah and Angelina Grimké in lecturing against slavery. Abby was even called a "menace to public morals." She became a special target for ministers, who went so far as to expel church members who listened to her. As a young woman Abby was a teacher, but she quit her job to give all of her time and energy to the antislavery movement. After Abby's marriage to Stephen S. Foster in 1845, both she and her husband became involved in the antislavery lecture circuit.

ERNESTINE POTOWSKI ROSE (1810-1892). "What right . . . has the law to intrust the interest and happiness of one being into the hands of another?" Ernestine Rose asked this question over and over again in the speeches she gave during the 1840s. Convinced that women must have a right to their own property, she devoted some eleven years to campaigning for the passage of the Married Woman's Property Act in New York State. A husband "*keeps* [his wife]," she told her audiences, "and so he does a favorite horse; by law they are both considered his property." Born in Poland, the daughter of a rabbi, young Ernestine defied tradition by declaring that she wanted to study Hebrew and the laws of the Torah. Such study was then reserved only for boys. When she was sixteen, Ernestine rebelled against a marriage that had been arranged for her, as was the custom of the day in Europe. Soon afterwards she left home, traveled widely, and married in England. She and her husband William Rose moved to the United States in 1836, where they both became involved in reform work.

ANNA HOWARD SHAW (1847-1919). Anna was not only a strong supporter of women's rights, but a preacher and a medical doctor as well. Her family emigrated from England when she was a child, settling first in Massachusetts and then in Michigan. She attended high school following the Civil War and went on to become an ordained minister of the Protestant Methodist Church in 1880. Just a few years later, she earned a medical degree at Boston University. It was while working as a doctor in the Bostom slums that she saw the plight of poor women and became involved in helping them. After she met Susan B. Anthony, she put much of her energy into the suffrage movement, eventually being elected president of the National American Woman Suffrage Association.

Suggested Reading

Clarke, Mary Stetson. *Bloomers and Ballots: Elizabeth Cady Stanton and Women's Rights*. New York: Viking Press, 1972. A detailed account of the life and work of Elizabeth Cady Stanton.

Gurko, Miriam. *The Ladies of Seneca Falls: The Birth of the Woman's Rights Movement*. New York: Macmillan, 1974. The history of the nineteenth-century woman's rights movement, with lively biographical material included.

Lester, Julius. *To Be A Slave*. New York: Dial Press, 1968; Dell, 1970. Collection of narratives of ex-slaves, ranging from accounts of their capture in Africa to their life after emancipation.

Nies, Judith. *Seven Women: Portraits from the American Radical Tradition*. New York: Viking Press, 1977. Contains chapters on Sarah Grimké and Elizabeth Cady Stanton.

Ortiz, Victoria. *Sojourner Truth, A Self-Made Woman*. Philadelphia: J. B. Lippincott, 1974. A good biography of the former slave and preacher.

Sterling, Dorothy. *Lucretia Mott, Gentle Warrior*. Garden City, New York: Doubleday, 1964. A fictional account of Mott's life.

Stevenson, Janet. *Women's Rights*. New York: Franklin Watts, 1972. Gallery of the pioneers for women's rights, with short histories accompanying the photographs.

Warren, Ruth. *A Pictorial History of Women in America*. New York: Crown Publishers, 1975. A survey of the accomplishments of American women from colonial days to the present.

Nancy Smiler Levinson is a free-lance magazine writer and the author of three children's books. Much interested in the lives and achievements of American women, she has previously written *Contributions of Women: Business* for Dillon Press.

Ms. Levinson earned a degree in journalism from the University of Minnesota and has worked both as a reporter and a book editor. Her articles have appeared in such publications as *Teen*, *Highlights for Children*, and *American Girl*. She and her husband live in Southern California and are the parents of two boys, Matthew and Danny.